Rider Haggard

Twayne's English Authors Series

Herbert Sussman, Editor
Northeastern University

TEAS 383

RIDER HAGGARD
(1856-1925)
Photo copyright by National Portrait Gallery, London

Rider Haggard

By Norman Etherington

University of Adelaide

Twayne Publishers • Boston

Rider Haggard

Norman Etherington

Copyright © 1984 by G. K. Hall & Company
All Rights Reserved
Published by Twayne Publishers
A Division of G. K. Hall & Company
70 Lincoln Street
Boston, Massachusetts 02111

Book Production by Marne B. Sultz

Book Design by Barbara Anderson

Printed on permanent/durable acid-free
paper and bound in the United States of America.

Library of Congress Cataloging in Publication Data

Etherington, Norman.
    Rider Haggard.

    (Twayne's English authors series; TEAS 383)
    Bibliography: p.
    Includes index.
    1. Haggard, H. Rider (Henry Rider), 1856-1925.
    2. Novelists, English—20th Century—Biography. I. Title.
    II. Series.
    PR4732.E86   1984   823'.8 [B]   83-22883
    ISBN 0-8057-6869-6

Dedicated to Marion Nell Etherington
who introduced me to books

Contents

About the Author

Norman Etherington was born in Port Townsend, Washington, in 1941 and graduated *summa cum laude* from Yale College in 1963. After completing his Ph.D. at Yale he joined the History Department at the University of Adelaide. He has served as chairman of the department and dean of the Faculty of Arts (1975—77). He has contributed articles on various aspects of African and British Imperial history to the *Journal of African History*, *Africa*, *Victorian Studies*, *History and Theory*, *Journal of Imperial and Commonwealth History*, *History of Political Economy*, *African Affairs*, *Meanjin Literary Quarterly*, and many other journals. He is the author of *Preachers, Peasants and Politics in Southeast Africa* (1978,) and *Theories of Imperialism: War, Capital, and Conquest* (1984) and has written portions of *The Anglo-Zulu War: New Perspectives* (1981). He has been a visiting fellow at the Institute of Commonwealth Studies (1974 and 1978) and senior visiting lecturer at the University of Cape Town (1981).

Preface

This is the first book length study of Rider Haggard's fiction. Three biographical works have been published since 1960 which testify to renewed interest in the man. Each struggles to explain two related problems: why have his first dozen "romances" retained a durable popularity and why were his later works scorned by readers of his own and later generations? None of the answers that have thus far been suggested provides a satisfactory explanation.

This study suggests that the answer is to be found in Haggard's use of the quest into unknown regions as a metaphor for the discovery of new facets of the human psyche in late Victorian England. As long as he stuck to that theme, he captivated both intellectuals and men on the street. When he strayed from it, his audience shrank drastically.

The interest of Haggard's work, however, extends far beyond the tales of African adventure that won him enduring fame. His writings on politics and agriculture illuminate important aspects of the mind of tory England at the dawning of the twentieth century. His peculiar brand of imperialism in politics and art needs to be understood before the complexities of British attitudes at the climax of imperial expansion can be adequately grasped. His attitudes towards women in the era of "the New Woman" also require closer study.

Rider Haggard achieved none of his dearest ambitions in literature, politics or agriculture. But he must not on that account be dismissed as a failure. He grappled with issues of great moment for our century in ways that are always interesting. His fantastic landscapes, lost kingdoms, immortal women, and mythic encounters between savage armies became the common property of twentieth-century image makers of both high and low culture.

This study began in 1969 in the reading rooms of the Natal Archives with a docket of papers concerning a black gardener who claimed to be the rightful ruler of the distant Ndebele kingdom. It received aid and encouragement from Jeff Guy of the University of Lesotho who possesses a wealth of knowledge about British colonialism and the Zulu people. Conversations in 1974 with Walter Reed of the English Department at the University of Texas at Austin helped uncover unsuspected links between Haggard and psychoanalytic theory. Peter Pierce, who returned to Australian literary studies after completing a thesis on Rider Haggard at Oxford in 1975, has helped at various stages by pointing out caches of published and unpublished material. Irene Cassidy of the Institute of Historical Research, University of London, ferreted out illustrations and newspaper clippings in England. Sonia Zabolocki deserves special thanks for typing initial and final drafts.

Chronology

1887 *She*, *Jess*, and *Allan Quatermain*. First trip to Egypt. Begins regular literary lunches at Saville Club with Andrew Lang, Walter Besant, and Edmund Gosse.

1888 *Colonel Quaritch V.G.* June-July, travels to Iceland.

1889 *Cleopatra.* 9 December, Mother dies.

1890 *The World's Desire*, written with Andrew Lang. *Eric Brighteyes*. Travels to Mexico.

1891 Devastated by death of son Jock. Ida Hector becomes his private secretary.

1892 *Nada the Lily.* 9 December, daughter Lilias born.

1893 *Montezuma's Daughter.* 22 April, father dies. Declines invitation to stand for parliament in King's Lynn.

1894 *People of the Mist.*

1895 Coeditor of *African Review*; gives up editorship before the Jameson Raid. Stands unsuccessfully for parliament. Elected to Athenaeum Club.

1896 *Heart of the World.*

1898 *A Farmer's Year.*

1899 *Swallow.*

1900 Travels to Italy and Middle East.

1902 *Rural England*, based on extensive travels with Arthur Cochrane to investigate the state of English agriculture.

1903 *Pearl Maiden.*

1905 *Ayesha.* Accepts commission from Rhodes trustees to report on the operation of Salvation Army "labour colonies" in North America.

1906 Becomes member of Royal Commission on Coast Erosion.

1908 *The Ghost Kings*, with a plot devised in collaboration with Rudyard Kipling.

1910 *Queen Sheba's Ring. Regeneration*, a defense of the Salvation Army.

1911 *The Mahatma and the Hare.*

1912   Knighted, joins Dominions Royal Commission, travels to Egypt. *Marie.*

1913   *Child of Storm*, based on Zulu history in consultation with Natal official James Stuart.

1914   Travels to South Africa and Canada with the Dominions Commission. Begins his diaries.

1916   Sent by Royal Colonial Institute to investigate prospects for "soldier settlers" in the Dominions. Gives up farming.

1917   *Finished.*

1918   *Moon of Israel.*

1919   Becomes involved in anti-Bolshevik movement.

1920   *The Ancient Allan. Smith and the Pharaohs.* Forms Liberty League to combat "Bolshevism" in Britain.

1921   *She and Allan.*

1925   January, Arthur Cochrane dies. 14 May Haggard dies of postoperative abcess.

1926   *Days of My Life*, posthumously published autobiography.

Chapter One
The Picture of Weakness and Dullness
Early Years in Norfolk and South Africa

Late in August 1875 General Sir Garnet Wolseley and his glittering retinue of brilliant officers handed over administration of the Natal Colony to Sir Henry Bulwer. The heroic veteran of the Crimea, Ashantiland, and half a score of other rugged adventures was not impressed by his replacements. He wrote in his diary that Bulwer's "only staff consists of a leggy youth not long I should say from school who seems the picture of weakness and dullness."[1] The leggy youth was Rider Haggard. Wolseley's opinion was shared by those who knew the boy best, including his own parents. His stern father and self-effacing mother had not thought him worthy of the financial sacrifices which would have been required to send him to Oxford or Cambridge where his older brothers had gone. He had mostly stayed at home on his family's Norfolk estate, reading much but keeping his thoughts to himself. Barely nineteen when he joined Bulwer in South Africa, Haggard had followed a mediocre career at school with failure in the army entrance exam and desultory private studies in London. He was tall and skinny and spoke with a lisp. No one, least of all himself, guessed that Africa was about to stir the vigorous imagination hid by his weak, dull exterior into extraordinary public activity, or that within a decade he would have written some of the most spectacularly successful novels to be published in late-Victorian England.

Explaining the reasons for that success is the principal aim of this book. No doubt, part of the explanation is to be found in Haggard's childhood and family experiences. His parents were not quite the conventional rural gentlefolk they seemed. Haggard's paternal grandfather had been a banker in Russia where he met and married a Russian Jew.[2] His mother's parents lived most of their lives on the distant island of St. Helena and in India. These exotic influences of

Britain's expanding empire were reinforced by his brothers, one of whom joined the navy, another the army, a third the diplomatic service, and a fourth the Indian civil service. All the children bore the impress of their parents. Father was a moody, blustering, explosive, frequently impossible personality. Mother was a quiet introvert with literary aspirations; her nine canto epic poem, *Myra, or the Rose of the East* was published the year after Rider's birth. The parental mix produced children with a reputation for instability. It was said that as late as the mid-twentieth century "tales of their scrapes and escapes, their eccentricities and extravagances, their dare-devil pranks and far from reputable love affairs" persisted in the neighborhood of Bradenham, West Norfolk.[3]

It is difficult to say to what extent the young Haggard himself participated in such escapades. Most of what is known about Rider Haggard's life and thought before he went out to Natal comes from his own pen.[4] In early adolescence he had dwelt with morbid melancholy on the inevitability of death and the terrors of hell. In his year of unrestrained freedom in London he had experimented with seances and fallen in love. The conventional notions of religion and morality which he had been taught as a boy on his stern father's Norfolk estate had been shaken by his reading of Comte, Hegel, and Darwin.[5] He felt strongly in his own bosom the tensions between morality and passion, science and religion, national independence and empire which dominated the thinking of his generation.

Now, in 1875, he was off to South Africa where those tensions were present on all sides in exaggerated form. It is impossible to overestimate the effect of South Africa on Haggard and his writing. Witnessing the confrontation between British colonialism and the Zulu people caused him to reappraise and define his thinking about the fundamental issues of sex, politics, and religion with which he would struggle in his future novels. The physical environment supplied the raw material for a thousand varied landscapes of the imagination.

Sir Henry Bulwer and his staff of one arrived at important moment in the development of the Natal Colony. The uneasy peace between the tiny population of white settlers and the subjugated black majority which had reigned for three decades had been broken two years earlier by the violent suppression of a recalcitrant petty chieftain.[6] General Wolseley had been dispatched by the Colonial Office with orders to curb the power of settler representatives to impose their own brutal notions of good government on Africans and also to pave the way for a confederation of South African states which would resolve perennial problems of defense, revenue, and labor supply which hampered the growth of "British civilization" in that corner of the empire. The possibilities for growth had recently been vastly expanded by the discovery of diamonds at Kimberley and gold to the east and north of the Transvaal Republic.

White and black Natalians were in the thick of these developments. Herbert and Cecil Rhodes gave up cotton farming to seek their fortunes at the diamond fields. Artist and explorer Thomas Baines went out to survey the mineral prospects to the north and came back with a map that depicted "gold bearing regions" in yellow circles which rise like expanding balloons toward the recently discovered " 'Simbaby'[Zimbabwe] ruins" and the "Supposed Realm of the Queen of Sheba" in central Africa. Agents of the London and Limpopo Mining Company seeking concessions from the Ndebele (Matabele) king Lobengula were given knowledgable African escorts by Natal's veteran Secretary for Native Affairs, Theophilus Shepstone. It was to Shepstone that Haggard gravitated more and more as his work for Sir Henry settled into lacklustei routine—Shepstone who seemed to Haggard the very embodiment of romantic imperialism. Shepstone, who sat like an enigmatic spider at the center of the web of Anglo-Zulu relations, seldom moving but constantly involved in grand political games for high stakes.[7]

Shepstone was also centrally concerned with the moral, religious, and philosophical issues which had perplexed the teenage Haggard. Shepstone's administration of the black population of Natal was based on the necessity for broad toleration for Zulu customs. The guiding principle of his understaffed administration of more than a hundred thousand Zulu subjects was rule through Zulu chiefs and "Native Law." He maintained the legal fiction that the British governor was paramount chief and that he, Shepstone, was the governor's chief *induna*. He surrounded himself with the trappings of Zulu kingship, presided over Zulu dances, and gave Zulu girls in marriage to his loyal black henchmen. Zulu praise singers chanted his biography on official occasions and shouted the royal salute *bayete* in his honor when he visited the neighboring Zulu kingdom. His administration condoned polygamy, bare breasts, and the unique Zulu form of mutual masturbation openly practiced by unmarried lovers. The idea of the Englishman who effortlessly and successfully rules over "savage" people as a savage chief would recur again and again in Haggard's fiction.

Shepstone left the Zulu people free to follow their own religious beliefs, until such time as they had voluntarily perceived the superior merits of Christianity. His long time partner in this program of toleration was the celebrated English bishop of Natal, J.W. Colenso. The bishop was an inquisitive broad churchman who believed that religious and scientific truth could be reconciled. He was an exponent of the ideas of Lyell and Darwin who had fought a long battle for his bishopric after a heresy trial in the 1860s. Not only did the bishop advocate tolerance of Zulu customs, he confessed that his own belief in the literal truth of the biblical account of creation had been shaken by the shrewd objections of one of his Zulu converts.[8] Although Colenso had broken off his friendship with Shepstone in 1874 because he could not approve of the harsh methods used to crush the petty chief Langalibalele, the Shepstone-Colenso approach to the encounter of British and Zulu culture was still very much alive as an idea when Haggard arrived in Natal.

Haggard went to hear Colenso preach and came away profoundly impressed by the bishop's intelligence, sincerity, and courage. Like Colenso, Haggard saw much of value in the Zulu social system and recognized the intellectual strength of the Zulu objections to Christian metaphysics. He especially noticed their complacent approach to death which they simply called "going down into the blackness"—so different from the combination of sickly sentimentality and cringing horror which enveloped the subject of death in Victorian culture. Another bishop had pronounced the Zulu to be the equal of "our European free thinkers" in debating ability. That picture of Zulu shrewdness would live on in Haggard's novels. So would an idealized picture of Shepstone's good government which protected the Zulu people from the rapacious greed of white settlers.

Haggard was too young and inexperienced to see the iron hand beneath the velvet glove of Shepstonian administration. Nor did he understand how Shepstone, while standing firm against the petty tyrannies of traders, farmers, and housewives, faithfully served the larger interests of big capital, mining developers, and sugar planters.[9] He embraced Shepstone as a surrogate father. He looked on Shepstone's veteran associates—especially Melmoth Osborn—as so many kindly uncles with endless stores of romantic tales of Africa and Africans. He jumped at the chance to join them on an adventurous mission to the Transvaal Republic in December 1876. Officially, Shepstone was simply fact-finding for the British government. Secretly, he carried instructions from London permitting him to annex and govern the republic as part of a Colonial Office scheme to confederate the states of South Africa. Haggard helped to raise the British flag over Pretoria in May 1877 and stayed on for two more years as Master and Registrar of the court in Shepstone's administration.

Those years were critical to Haggard's personal development in ways that his published reminiscences only hint at. In Natal his intellect and imagination had been stimulated by the challenges of Shepstone's politics, Colenso's religion, and the Zulu culture. In Pretoria, with an official position and an assured income, he was free to live much as he wished, according to whatever values he could distil from the conflicting examples which life had so far presented to him. His first instinct was to marry. Early in 1877 he made plans to return to England bearing private messages from Shepstone to the colonial secretary and from himself to Mary Elizabeth Archer, the young lady he had met at a ball in London two years before. However, his father reprimanded him so severely for this disruption of a promising public career that he hastily abandoned his plan. A few months later he received a letter informing him that the lady was to marry another man. He blamed his father bitterly for this disappointment. He brooded on the shattered romance with a melancholy intensity matched only by his continued preoccupation with the inevitability of death. He made the most of what bachelor life had to offer in the spirited company of another young official, Arthur Cochrane. Together they built a house, talked of going ostrich farming, and had affairs.[10]

English gentlemen had no difficulties finding women in Natal or Pretoria. General Wolseley observed that his men would go back to England singing of *"the wives"* they left behind them. The rawness of sexual life in frontier towns was perpetually on display in the newspapers and the courts.[11] In the slums and shanty-towns, white and black cohabited with a freedom that would be unknown a few decades later. The shock which young Haggard felt in the presence of atheists who openly flaunted their desires, fearing no eternal punishments, would be set down a few years later in his partly autobiographical novel *Jess*.

His political credo also developed during the years in Pretoria. No sooner had Shepstone annexed the Transvaal than the whole confederation scheme began to fall apart. The annexation stirred nationalist feelings among the Boer population throughout South Africa. Plots of rebellion grew rife in the Transvaal as Shepstone proved himself incapable of delivering the sound, solvent administration he had promised. Lord Carnarvon, the architect of confederation, resigned as colonial secretary and his chief deputy, High Commissioner Sir Bartle Frere plunged into a series of unwise, unsuccessful wars against independent black kingdoms. The war against the Zulus began in January 1879 with a spectacular defeat for the British forces at Isandhlwana.[12] Shock waves from that and other imperial disasters brought down Disraeli's Conservative government in the British general election of 1880. Gladstone was swept into office on a tide of popular revulsion against "imperialism." Within two years his government had dismantled all the scaffolding of confederation which Carnarvon, Shepstone, and Frere had painstakingly erected. Instead of annexing Zululand, Gladstone broke the conquered territory into thirteen petty chieftaincies which predictably began to bicker and fight. When the disaffected Boers of the Transvaal rebelled, Gladstone negotiated the return of their independence.

Haggard watched these events with increasing consternation. In May 1879 he left the sinking ship of Shepstone's administration and went into ostrich farming in northern Natal with Arthur Cochrane. Taking advantage of this break in his career to make a trip to England, he arrived home in time to observe the whole of the general election campaign and Gladstone's vilification of everything he had been working for in South Africa. It bred in him a permanent dislike of parliamentary democracy and party politics. If the fickleness of the electorate could overturn in an instant the foundations of a great African empire which had been years in the making, Haggard would prefer to keep the business of government well away from their hands. He remained a Tory for the rest of his life.

This trip to England settled the marriage question as well as the political question. Louisa Margitson, the orphaned daughter of an army officer and heiress to a modest Norfolk estate, came to stay with his sister Mary and within a week said yes to Haggard's proposal. She was engaged before she could spell his name properly.[13] Complications ensued when her guardians refused to consent to marriage before she had legally come of age. The couple impetuously decided to fight their case in the courts, even though they had less than a year to wait before Louisa's twenty-first birthday. They won, but the battle cost £3,000 in legal expenses and left Haggard with a lasting contempt for the pettifogging procedures of Victorian courts. Lawyers both villainous and humorous figure prominently in his early realistic novels, as do fights for estates.

By all accounts Louisa made Haggard a practical, dutiful wife. But she was not the romantic heroine of his fantasies. His daughter Lilias paints an unflattering picture of her mother as an outwardly cold person, incapable of showing love to her children or her husband. Haggard's nephew Godfrey reinforces the impression that Louisa was not "the perfect mate, whose general characteristics may be gathered from the collective heroines of his romances."[14] She became his companionable "Louie" but never succeeded in making him forget the promise and disappointment of his first great love.

In November 1880 they set off together for the ostrich farm in Natal. A few months later their son was born. Life with the temperamental ostriches proved to be an unequal contest which Haggard was unwilling to continue as the political situation deteriorated. The outbreak of the Transvaal rebellion brought war to his immediate neighborhood. The hapless British general Colley suffered decisive defeat only a few miles away at Majuba, and Haggard's farm was let for a few weeks to the high commissioner who came up from Cape Town to negotiate the terms of peace. All this was too much. Physically afraid of being discovered by the Boers as one of the men who had raised the Union Jack over Pretoria, he wound up the partnership with Cochrane and took his family back to England in the autumn of 1881. There he embarked on an entirely new career. Living on his wife's income from the rental of her estate, he suppressed his distaste for lawyers and began to read for the bar at Lincoln's Inn.

Haggard Becomes a Writer

In his spare time he wrote contemporary history. His first book, *Cetywayo and His White Neighbours* (June 1882) is a carefully researched vindication of British policy in South Africa.[15] Based on a mountain of official papers, it shows just how good Haggard was at extracting the vital elements from complex materials and marshaling them in support of a convincing partisan argument. The preeminent modern historian of this period in Zulu history has called *Cetywayo and His White Neighbours* "an extremely lucid, cleverly presented statement of Shepstone's point of view on South African affairs."[16] It indicates what Haggard might have done had he persevered either with government service or the law. It also gives an insight into Haggard's personal brand of colonialism. He argued that the division of Zululand into thirteen quarreling chieftaincies was a mistake. Since the kingdom could not be put together again, it should be ruled on Shepstonian lines by enlightened British administrators. The

Transvaal should be ruled by the British in order to prevent the Boers from abusing the blacks. He disagreed with the prevailing opinion "that the white man has a right to the black man's possessions and land, and that it is his high and holy mission to exterminate the wretched native and take his place." His own experience was "that in all the essential qualities of mind and body they very much resemble white men, with the exception that they are, as a race, quicker-witted, more honest, and braver than the ordinary run of white men." It appeared to him "that on only one condition, if at all, have we the right to take the black men's land; and that is, that we provide them with an equal and a just Government, and allow no maltreatment of them, either as individuals or tribes, but, on the contrary, do our best to elevate them, and wean them from savage customs. Otherwise, the practice is surely indefensible" (269—70).

Cetywayo did not sell well, though it was gratefully received by Carnarvon and Shepstone. That, however, did not deter Haggard from beginning another book a few months later. He and his wife had both been overwhelmed by the singular beauty of a stranger seen one Sunday at church. They resolved that each would make up a story about the unknown 'Angela." Louie's story was abandoned after a few pages but Haggard's became the novel *Dawn*. This strange amalgam of gothic romanticism and realism was rejected by several publishers before Haggard sought advice on his manuscript from an established author, Cordy Jeaffreson.[17] Jeaffreson took a kindly interest in the work, praised it for flashes of inspiration, but urged Haggard "not to publish it in its present rude form." Whereupon Haggard sat down to do something he would never do again; he carefully rewrote the book from start to finish over four months in 1883. With Jeaffreson's letter of recommendation, *Dawn* found a publisher. The *Times* praised it as "a striking and original novel." His literary career was launched. Another novel, *The Witch's Head* partly set in South Africa, was finished within a few months and published in 1884.

Meanwhile, he persevered with his legal studies, still indebted to his wife for a very modest income. Aside from references in his autobiography to his straitened circumstances and his efforts to establish himself as an author, little is known about Haggard's daily life between his return to England in 1881 and his admission to the bar in January 1885. His companionable marriage appears to have been at its happiest. Two daughters were born in rapid succession during 1883 and 1884. Both were named for heroines of his novels, the first after the ethereal Angela, the second, after the practical Dolly of *The Witch's Head,* who bears a marked resemblance to Louie. At the same time, there were hints in *Witch's Head* of the love triangle which would recur in most of the later novels. The young hero gives up the shining beauty of his dreams to another and reconciles himself to married life with a plain, solid, sensible alternative; at the same time he feels that he is still bound to the first woman, if not in this life, then in some future one. The sexual longing that would never be satisfied remained a leitmotiv of Haggard's life as well as his fiction.

His ambitions for money and fame, on the other hand, were satisfied quickly as the result of four novels written during the fourteen months which followed his admission to the Bar. The first and most famous was *King Solomon's Mines,* a story of African adventure for boys done in deliberate imitation of Robert Louis Stevenson's *Treasure Island.* He boasted in his autobiography that it was written in six weeks. His jotting book for 1885 records that it was begun in January and finished on the 21 April.[18] In any case it was a remarkable performance, similar in many ways to Stevenson's feat in dashing off *Dr. Jekyll and Mr. Hyde* after a vivid dream in the same year. Both Haggard and the reading public recognized the parallel between Stevenson's work and his own.[19] Critics treated them as harbingers of a new trend in literature which they called "romance." Thirty-one thousand copies of *King Solomon's Mines* were sold in England alone within a year of its publication—a figure which put it among the hottest best-sellers of the time. Similar records were run up by the books which followed, *Allan Quatermain* written in the summer of 1885, *Jess,* written in the autumn of the same year, and *She,* written between January and March 1886. All four books were set in Africa, drawing heavily on Haggard's experiences and the tales he had heard there.

His jotting books for the same year reveal, however, that a flood of ideas for other stories in other settings was welling up from somewhere inside him: "Sketch of a story, Idea of a mental vampire in shape of a woman sucking the life out of man who worships her"; "Story of a man working away whilst his pretty wife runs here and there and finally deserts him"; "Tale of a suicide epidemic"; "Tale of dead drowned man met in the Strand"; "Reflections on the condition of the World when religion has died out of it, and poverty been suspended by adoption of the Malthusian theory, and so of crime . . . hopelessness and calm . . . war at end"; "Idea of a dual identity or transference of the spirit (to be worked out)"; "Witch Story. Woman in cave. fire w. eye out. Curse Him. It is well to put out an eye . . .

Fetish Dance of all the people dressed up like animals. Raising the dead. Casket washed up. Classic Swahili''; "Story. Oasis in the Ice at the North Pole a relic civilization of extinct continent''; "Story of Mesmerism''; "Story of a man w head off''; "Story of a devil''; "Idea of white women brought up by Malays.''[20]

This list is vivid evidence of a mind brimming over with ideas. With a ready market available for anything he cared to write, he could at last reveal the extraordinarily original imagination whose existence had been hitherto concealed from almost everyone who knew him. Half a dozen literary genres compete for Haggard's attention on that list. There is realism with an emphasis on adultery. There are tales of horror, insanity, and the supernatural. There is time travel into the past to view ancient civilizations, and into the future to view brave new worlds. Interspersed among them is the reiterated theme of dual identities, whether revealed under hypnosis, in a "transference of the spirit," or in the transformation of people into animals. It was indeed a theme "to be worked out." With plenty of money behind him, Haggard could give up the law and pursue it.

He established himself as gentleman farmer in Norfolk and as a man of letters in London. Louie's estate at Ditchingham was reclaim-ed from the tenants and stocked with animals, craftsmen, and ser-vants. On Saturdays Haggard went to literary lunches at London's Saville Club with a small group of like-minded authors, the most famous of whom were Walter Besant, Edmund Gosse, and Haggard's champion Andrew Lang. As English editor of *Harper's* magazine and an influential critic, Lang was in a position to do Haggard a great deal of good. They formed a close friendship based on mutual professional needs. Haggard found in Lang a wise and learned advisor who oc-cupied in his literary life the position Shepstone had filled in his earlier career in government service. Lang looked to Haggard (and Stevenson) to write the books which would make "romance" a move-ment capable of storming the literary heights then commanded by realism and naturalism.[21] He supplied Haggard with ideas for plots based on his extensive studies of comparative mythology. He recognized Haggard as a man who was putting the lessons of contem-porary anthropology to work in the service of literature. He added his voice to others who hoped that Haggard would develop a style worthy of his remarkable imagination. (One reviewer said that he expressed conceptions worthy of Dante in language comparable to the *Daily Telegraph*.) When Haggard objected that "the stuff," that is the ideas expressed in his books, was what counted most, Lang replied,

"*Of course* I know the stuff is the thing, but the ideal thing would be the perfection of stuff and the perfection of style, and we don't often get that."[22]

Haggard listened to some of this advice, but with a string of vastly successful books behind him he was increasingly inclined to trust his own judgment. He considered speed to be a virtue rather than a defect. *She* had been written "at a white heat, almost without rest, and that," he held, "is the best way to compose."[23] In 1887 he was unwise enough to publish an article, "About Fiction," which offered a whole series of similar slapdash judgments on the writer's craft.[24] At the same time that it damned three quarters of all books written as worthless, it praised "good romance writing" as "perhaps the most difficult art practiced by the sons of man." Haggard had set himself up to be knocked down. His critical reputation never fully recovered from the taunts and jeers which the article provoked. Lang's hope that he would be the new Walter Scott to set romance on the pinnacle of critical esteem were dashed at the same time; Lang's own reputation suffered in the backlash. The upshot was that the supersensitive Haggard henceforth deliberately distanced himself from the literary establishment. He would not read their books and professed not to care if they read his. His alternative role as Norfolk country squire and sometime African adventurer gave him a respectable cover for his defensive attitude. He would say publicly that "at the bottom of my heart I share some of the British contempt for the craft of story-writing."[25] But the private hurt cut deep. It stunted his development as an artist, helping to ensure that almost nothing that he subsequently wrote would match the success of the romances written before 1887. He continued to write as quickly as before, almost inviting people to say that he only did it for the money.

There are many reasons to regret the uproar over Haggard's little article. In addition to the lifelong pain it gave him, it prevented serious discussion of the important issues he had tried to raise. His purpose was not to glorify his own literary achievements but to explain why he had chosen to express himself through the medium of fantasies. He began with the proposition that the spread of education had created an enormous body of readers who longed to be edified and improved through literature less demanding than the works of truly great writers such as Thackeray and George Eliot. As he put it, "they long to be brought face to face with Beauty, and stretch their arms towards that vision of the Perfect, which we only see in books and dreams." He singled out three contemporary schools of literature which competed for the attention of this middling sort of audience. One school produced drawing-room romances about insipid people with anemic emotions. Another, the school of naturalism best represented by Emile Zola in France, went to the opposite extreme of showing physical passion in the raw. Haggard acknowledged the power of this literature. "Sexual passion" was undoubtedly "the most powerful lever with which to stir the mind of man, for it lies at the root of all things human." The trouble with French naturalism was that it aroused erotic instincts which inevitably debased rather than elevated readers—"once start the average mind upon this subject, and it will go down the slope of itself." Finally, there was fiction produced in England which expressly excluded anything which could not safely be read by young girls under sixteen years of age.

Haggard felt sure that if prudish censors attempted to confine all fiction within that namby-pamby barrier there would be a backlash among adult readers "and Naturalism in all its horror will take root among us." People would soon be reveling in "the inner mysteries of life in brothels" and "the passions of senile and worn-out debauchees." Their eagerness to read court reports in the sensational newspapers proved that they would fall readily into the arms of the pornographers. (Haggard gave as an example the three-in-a-bed scandal which had ruined Sir Charles Dilke.) He contended that a new form of fiction was needed which would deal with the human realities of sex and violence without titillating or degrading readers. That fiction, he argued, would move in the realms of "pure imagination." There are, he concluded, "still subjects that may be handled there if the man can be found bold enough to handle them." He thus invited readers to consider his own fiction on two levels. On the surface it simply entertained and pointed a "harmless moral." At another level it dealt with eternal truths and the deepest human urges. This was the honest artistic credo of a reticent man who longed to explore the moral dilemmas confronting ordinary people in a Darwinian universe—the dilemmas which Haggard had personally confronted in Africa but which he was temperamentally incapable of writing about in a straightforward, open fashion.

His travels abroad attest to the interest he maintained in improving his work even after his rejection by the literary establishment. Already a master at conjuring up imaginary landscapes, he went to Iceland, to Mexico, to the Middle East, and to Denmark in search of more material. And he went again and again to Egypt which was the ultimate source of all his tales of ancient civilizations. As he made the rounds of ancient temples, burial caves, and battlegrounds, the conviction grew within him that these sites of public history were actually parts of his private past, that in "previous lives" he had visited them. This conviction gradually fused with his belief that the loves and friendships of his present existence were immortal entanglements which continued from life to life over the course of innumerable centuries.[26] At the same time that he professed these beliefs with the deepest religious intensity, he held somewhere in his mind the equally insistent alternative propositions that life had no meaning and that death ended all. His fictional character Allan Quatermain puts it like this:

At one time we are all spiritual; at another all physical; at one time we are sure that our lives here are as a dream and a shadow and that the real existence lies elsewhere; at another that these brief days of ours are the only business with which we have to do and that of it we must make the best. At one time we think our loves much more immortal than the stars; at another that they are mere shadows cast by the baleful sun of desire upon the shallow and fleeting water we call Life which seems to flow out of nowhere into nowhere.[27]

The tension between these extreme points of view added interest to Haggard's romances but stood in the way of any simple-minded enjoyment of "shadows cast by the baleful sun of desire." The closest he came to levity about sex in any of his writings is this little verse from his jotting book for 1885:

> Holy Mother we believe
> Without sin thou didst conceive
> Holy Mother thus believing
> May we sin without conceiving[28]

Did he? The strong probability is that he did, in the late 1880s, have one or more adulterous affairs. It is certain that he reopened contacts with his first great love whose marriage had proved to be both financially and romantically disastrous. His fascination with her did not wear off, to the undoubted discomfort of his family who did their best to adjust to her presence in his life. Haggard's daughter Lilias thought her a "gentle and rather stupid character" whose attraction was diabolically incomprehensible; she names her "Lilith" after the apocryphal witch of Genesis.[29] Whether this or any other relationship was consummated physically is not terribly important. The subject was constantly on his mind. The temptations and perils of adultery dominate Haggard's realistic novels beginning with *Beatrice* (1890). Star-crossed lovers trapped in unhappy marriages sometimes do and sometimes do not give in to temptation. Whatever the outcome, the temptation is always there.

Haggard's brooding on this subject increased after a crisis in his marriage in the early 1890s. Just before leaving on a treasure-hunting expedition to Mexico in January 1891, he experienced a strong premonition that he would never see his son Jock again. Although hardly a day went by in Haggard's life without some sort of gloomy premonition, in this case the feeling was justified. In February, Jock died suddenly from complications following an attack of measles. Haggard was inconsolable. "Then," he wrote later, "in truth I descended into Hell."[30] He secretly believed that the child's death was divine retribution for his own carnal sins.[31] Nevertheless, he believed that the impulse to promiscuity was present by nature in all men. "Nature," he reflected, "says to Everyman who is a man: "See where She stands with longing arms and lips that murmur love. . . . 'Touch not, taste not, handle not,' answers the cold stern Law, 'Pass on, she is not thine.' " Nonetheless, "often enough it is Nature that prevails and, having eaten of the fruit that She, our Mother, gives us, we desire no other fruit. But always the end is the same: its sweetness turns to gravel in our mouth. Shame comes, sorrow comes; come death and separations. And greater than all of these, remorse rises in the after years and stands over us at night. . . ."[32] Black depression and hypochondria followed Jock's death. He wrote very little. An attempt to fill the gap left by Jock produced another daughter, Lilias (born December 1892), who grew up believing that her father resented her for not being a boy and that her mother resented her for having been born at all.[33] Her opinion was that her mother broke off all sexual relations with Rider in order to avoid having any more unwanted children.

Adding to Haggard's disappointment was the unabating hostility which most serious critics showed toward his writing. "It was," he recorded bitterly, "the fashion to attack me in those days." He even came to agree with them, judging that the best he could "do in the lines of romance and novel-writing" was "to be found among the first dozen or so books" he had written, "say between *King Solomon's Mines* [1885] and *Montezuma's Daughter*."[34] When he finally emerged from his long period of depression, he turned his attention away from literature toward politics and agriculture.

He was elected chairman of his local bench of magistrates and, in 1893, was invited to contest the parliamentary seat of King's Lynn. He declined that invitation because of the expenses involved, but began to write and speak more frequently on public affairs, particularly in relation to Africa. This brought him to the attention of the South African financial interests clustered around Cecil Rhodes and the gold mining magnates of the Witwatersrand. They encouraged him to stand for another Norfolk constituency in the general election of 1895, and set him up as coeditor of a new journal called the *African Review* with offices in London's banking district. In his autobiography Haggard writes of this period with evident embarrassment.[35] He, who had put into the mouth of one of his early fictional heroes a pretty speech about refusing to hand over a beautiful piece of Africa "to be torn and fought over by speculators, tourists, politicians and teachers," was now the intimate associate of the despoilers of Matabeleland and the wire-pullers of the stock exchange.[36] The boom in South African gold shares was at its height with fortunes being made and lost every day. It was not so much the unsavory nature of his work in London as the nerve-racking ups and downs of the marketplace that caused him to pull out of the whole business after nine months. He counted himself lucky to have got out just before the failure of Dr. Jameson's raid on the Transvaal brought the whole gang of South African politician-financiers into general disrepute. Though he spoke in defense of the raid, his opinion of Rhodes and his minions was markedly lower than that of most people who shared Haggard's faith in Tory imperialism. When his bid for election to parliament failed by 198 votes, he was happy to hide his disappointment under the convenient cover of the country gentleman's traditional contempt for money-grubbers and politicians.

He was, however, quite unlike the typical gentleman farmer in his approach to agriculture. After a thorough scientific and economic study, he concluded that English agriculture was in the process of being ruined by an outmoded system of land tenure and unfair competition from overseas producers. In *A Farmer's Year* (1898) he set down a record of his own small triumphs and frustrations. Three years later, he traveled the length and breadth of the country with his old South African partner Arthur Cochrane, collecting data for a comprehensive survey of English agriculture. The result, *Rural England* (1902), was widely acclaimed as the best book on the subject since Arthur Young's similar survey in the eighteenth century.[37] At the heart of *Rural England* was a Tory argument as old as the Romans and familiar to readers of Haggard's novels: that the future greatness of the nation depended on the maintenance of a sturdy yeomanry in the countryside. Government neglect of agriculture had driven millions of people off the land into crowded, unhealthy cities. It had threatened national defense by making it impossible for Britain to feed her people in the event of a major war. *Rural England* gave Haggard an instant reputation as an expert on environmental questions whose aid was sought by all kinds of reformers from the radical right to the moderate left. The New Town movement welcomed him as a supporter of their crusade for the creation of urban environments which integrated city and countryside.[38] The trustees of Cecil Rhodes's estate commissioned him to investigate the success of a Salvation Army scheme to settle impoverished city dwellers on farms in the United States and Canada.[39] A Liberal government appointed the former Conservative candidate to a royal commission on coast erosion and afforestation in 1906. Another Liberal government knighted him and made him a member of the Dominions Royal Commission in 1912.

These honors and public commissions caused him to wonder more and more whether he had made the right decision when he gave up the law and government service to write fiction. Nevertheless, he continued to write novels at a rate slightly better than one a year. Some of these took the public's favorite characters—Allan Quatermain, Ayesha, and Umslopogaas into new adventures. Some were plotted in conversations with Rudyard Kipling who became a closer friend as their literary reputations sank together in the twilight of empire.[40] An ambitious trilogy (*Marie, Child of Storm* and *Finished*) traced in fiction the rise and fall of the Zulu monarchy. Meanwhile he scribbled in his jotting books the plots of realistic novels which mostly remained unwritten, but which expressed his continuing dissatisfaction with the constraints of respectable marriage. For example,

A is married unhappily and has a Lady friend B. To her he goes for consolation and she becomes attached to him. In the end at some crisis such as the death of his child [!] he declares his passion. She takes time to reflect then deliberately becomes his mistress. Note she is . . . an advanced woman. There is a character who warns her against this step telling her that no sin prospers and her evil will find her out (. . . a calvinistic parson). She answers with the usual arguments. He answers that her view is mistaken and earth is not *meant* to be pleasant and a heaven. This touches her latent religious fibre but she perseveres. For a while she is happy notwithstanding shifts and insults and has a child. Then the wife dies and she expects A will marry her. He is most anxious to do so but his passion has cooled a little—but she is not quite as handsome as she was—but such a step would ruin him! A most desirable match presents itself to A. He goes for it, afterwards circumstances change and he comes back to B and wants to marry her. She refuses both on grounds of pride and piety. All this to be worked out.[41]

But of course he never did work it out. In 1909 his old love ''Lilith'' died a horridly lingering death in sight of the Haggard family, her later years having been thoroughly blighted by her miserable husband. One of Haggard's ways of coping with this and other disappointments was to insist with increased fervor on the truth of reincarnation. The idea which he had first tentatively expressed in the *Witch's Head,* that lovers worked out their relationships in successive lives and literally eternal triangles, became a dominant theme in his later novels. He believed that he had caught glimpses of his own previous existences in dreams and visions. While writing his autobiography in 1912, he claimed to have had four of these recurring visions. In the first he is a young man dressed in skins at a cooking fire in a setting very like the Bath Hills of England. In the second he is a black man fending off an attack on his black family. An Egyptian palace is the setting of the third, in which he greets a furtive lover with violet eyes. A slightly taller version of Violet Eyes crops up in the fourth fantasy. She leaps up from her seat in a Viking hall and throws her sobbing self on Haggard's armor-clad breast.

There is something more than faintly ridiculous about these ''visions.'' They might be tableaux from the ethnographic section of a museum. He arranges them in the chronological order which an Edwardian museum director might have arranged displays on ''the ascent of man'' from the Stone Age to the Iron Age. They might also, of course, be scenes from Haggard's novels. However, he treated them as serious scientific phenomena to be explained, offering three hypotheses of his own. They could be either the products of his ''subconscious imagination'' or *''racial* memories'' or ''memories of some central incident that occurred in a previous incarnation.''[42] He preferred the third hypothesis which he used to support a reworking of orthodox Christian beliefs. Arguing that God would not be so unfeeling as to damn men forever for sins of the flesh committed in the hot-blooded youth of a single life, Haggard advanced the theory that the moral perfection demanded of Christians was to be achieved over the courses of several successive existences.[43] This belief may have salved his own oversensitive conscience but it did little to improve the

popularity of his novels, which grew more and more mystical.
Whatever the reasons, Haggard's later fiction did not sell very well.
This reinforced his feeling that he was out of tune with his age. He
often said that the compressed excitement of his early adulthood had
prematurely aged him. Youthful success and his proclivity for befrien-
ding older men like Shepstone and Osborn, who were always dying
off, increased his morbid sense of time fleeting. He felt old at thirty-
five. His autobiography, written when he was fifty-five, is full of
asides about his decrepitude. His diaries, begun at outbreak of World
War I and intended for eventual publication as a private testament of
that global conflagration, became the rambling monologue of a lonely, disappointed man. At first he welcomed the war, believing that it
would vindicate the moral worthiness of his earlier writing. "For
years," he wrote, "the subject of war has been more or less taboo in
England. For instance how often have I been attacked for writing
stories that deal with fighting rather than with sexual complications."
War was bringing home some "elementary facts" expounded in his
books, which had been formerly considered "to be so infinitely inferior" to the productions of the pacifically inclined Oscar Wilde and
George Bernard Shaw.[44] As late as July 1917, he wrote proudly that
England had become "very martial. Three years ago we were a nation
of trading civilians, who screamed at the very word conscription.
Now, behold, an armed camp or rather a nation in arms and everyone
(practically) content to have it so."[45] On the other hand, his eager offers to serve in a military or civilian capacity were politely rebuffed. He
was too old. The final episode in his public career as the advocate of
national regeneration through agriculture came in 1916 when he was
sent by the Royal Colonial Institute to investigate the prospects for
settling war veterans on plots of land in South Africa, Australasia, and
Canada. He gave up active farming the following year.

    The wave of revulsion against war and imperialism, which swept
England when the maimed survivors of the trenches did at last come
home, made Haggard feel more cut off than ever from the younger
generation. He reacted violently when a postwar president of the Oxford Union claimed that "if you wish to see what young men think of
war today you will not find their opinion in any of the Romantics or
the Victorians. You will not find it in the flamboyant insolence of
Rudyard Kipling. . . . . You will find it in the verse of Siegfried Sassoon." Haggard commented without embarrassment, "I am not for-
tunate enough to be acquainted with the works of Siegfried Sassoon,
who, from his name, I presume is a Jew of the advanced school."[46]

He wondered where the Sassoons and Sitwells were leading England, but did not read their works. During the same period, his diaries record numerous examples of the impertinence and irresponsibility of the young. His undisguised feeling that the country was going to the dogs made him ready prey for propagandists preaching the dangers of the "Red Menace."

In April 1919 he was recruited to Admiral Sir Reginald Hall's National Propaganda which aimed to awaken people to the true meaning of Bolshevism. He was soon seeing Reds under all the beds. A "Secret venom" was "being injected into the honest blood of Britain by foreign anarchists." The "unemployment dole" was "rotting this country to the bone." When Kipling expressed the opinion "that we owe all our Russian troubles, and many others, to the machinations of the Jews," Haggard replied that he personally was "inclined to read Trade Unions instead of Jews." Perhaps, he suggested, the two of them should write to the *Times* "setting out this Bolshevist business clearly and trying to arouse the country to a sense of all its horrors." By March 1920 he was immersed in the affairs of another anti-Bolshevik organization, the Liberty League. This turned out as badly as his flirtation with South African speculators in the 1890s. The secretary absconded with the funds and Lord Northcliffe, proprietor of the *Times*, who had done a great deal to stir up the red scare in the first place, now declared his belief that there was no Bolshevism in England. Haggard narrowly escaped being held up to public ridicule.[47]

Thus he maintained in his final years the extraordinary duality that had marked him from childhood. If the outward self was no longer "the picture of weakness and dullness," it was nevertheless thoroughly conventional. To the world at large he appeared as the bluff squire-writer, boring the pants off people with his cantankerous opinions about trade unions, Reds, the avant-garde, and the empire. In the recesses of his imagination, however, and in the company of his few intimate acquaintances, he pondered endlessly the profoundest questions of morals and metaphysics. He clambered on the stony outcrops of weird landscapes after visions of other lives, lost wisdom, and immortal loves, keeping one eye always fixed on the ever-present abyss of nothingness below. On the happy occasion that he did encounter someone who understood and shared his general view of life, the habitual reticence fell entirely away. In 1916 he spent an exhilarating day with ex-President Theodore Roosevelt whose "burning manner of speech" Haggard found "nervous in its intensity." "And

Heaven, how we talked! Of all sorts of things; of the world and its affairs, of religion, of heaven and hell, of the fundamental truths, and the spirit of man; for when men like Roosevelt and myself meet—men who are in deep and almost mysterious sympathy with one another, there are many vital matters on which we need to know each other's mind.''[48]

Such moments were rare in his old age because death had snatched away so many of his soul mates. We have the testimony of his daughter, however, that his last years were happier than many that had gone before.[49] His domestic life was calmer now that secret longings and love affairs were left behind. (He observed in his diary that there seemed to be fewer beautiful women about than in the days of his youth.)[50] Earnings from his novels continued to decline, but offsetting the hurt of his sunken reputation as an author was the burgeoning popularity of his work among moviemakers. The strongly visual character of his novels made them readily transferable to celluloid. No fewer than seven versions of *She* were produced in his lifetime.[51] Having spent so much of that lifetime in the company of Death, he did not shrink from its near approach. In May 1925 a postoperative infection carried him away. The death-bed scene was curiously apt, as though the soul within had at last visibly escaped from its crusty chrysalis. His matter-of-fact son-in-law Major Cheyne was with him. ''The window-blind was up, and the blaze from a large building on fire was visible in the distance. Rider rose up in bed, and pointed to the conflagration with arm outstretched, the red glow upon his dying face. 'My God!' said Cheyne to himself, 'an old Pharaoh!' ''[52]

Chapter Two
Attempts at Realism

Haggard's Fiction

In accordance with contemporary nomenclature Rider Haggard divided his fiction into two broad categories. The books he called novels were set in contemporary England. Those he called romances contained some element of fantasy and were set in previous ages or distant continents. There is a sharp contrast between the early novels and romances. They differ vastly in tone as well as setting. The novels won little acclaim. The romances made Haggard a wealthy man. In order to understand the reasons for the contrasting fortunes of the novels and romances, it will be useful to consider them in relation to Haggard's exemplars in each genre—the books he most admired and strove after his own fashion to imitate. When Haggard wrote of books that influenced or moved him, two always stood at the top of his list. One was the bleak *Story of an African Farm* which Olive Schreiner published under the pen name of Ralph Iron in 1884. The other was Robert Louis Stevenson's fantasy *Dr. Jekyll and Mr. Hyde* first published in 1885. This chapter will suggest reasons why Haggard achieved only mediocrity in his attempts at realism after the fashion of Olive Schreiner. The following chapter will attempt to explain why he succeeded marvelously in his stories of fantasy and adventure when he set off in the footsteps of Stevenson.

Haggard and Olive Schreiner

It is not difficult to see why he liked *Story of an African Farm*. The author was his contemporary and the setting was the South Africa he had known in the 1870s. The problems faced by the main characters were problems which centrally concerned him. The book opens with a scene remarkably similar to his own first awakening to the fact of death. A little boy, Waldo, lies awake in the dark listening to the ticking of a watch. "And every time it ticked *a man died!*" "He saw before him a long stream of people, a great dark multitude, that moved in one direction; then they came to the dark edge of the world and went over.'' Traditional religion gives him no comfort. He is half an atheist even before books of biblical criticism and natural history underpin the foundations of his disbelief. A chance encounter with an educated skeptic (modeled on one of the Shepstone family) shows him that people in the wider world share his perceptions.[1] There is no God. Good triumphs as often as bad. Sensual pleasures offer only temporary relief for thirsty souls. Truth is despised by the swinish multitude and is beyond the reach of the aspiring few. On the same farm live two sisters, one plain and practical, the other, beautiful and intellectual. Lyndall, the beauty, feels the ironies of existence as keenly as Waldo. She returns from finishing school worldly-wise, forlornly cynical, and pregnant. She will not compromise her feminist principles by marrying the object of a purely physical passion. And, though she is revolted by the doglike attentions of her sister's effeminate ex-fiancé , she flirts with the idea of a marriage of convenience to legitimize her child. In the end she dies alone, somewhat ennobled by suffering but otherwise unfulfilled and unenlightened. The central characters make their pointless pilgrimages to the grave through a typically spacious South African landscape in the company of poor whites, black servants, gentlemen treasure-seekers, and ignorant Boer pastoralists.

Rider Haggard wrote incessantly about those same themes and landscapes. The contrasted sisters are straight out of his cabinet of stock devices. Jiltings, adulteries, and illegitimacies are the principal problems which plague the heroes and heroines of his realistic novels. Doubts about God and the hereafter are always present. But Haggard never combined these elements in a novel fit to stand alongside Olive Schreiner's classic. After a few attempts he stopped trying. Some of the reasons for his relative failure in this genre are apparent in his first attempts at fiction, *Dawn* and *The Witch's Head*.

First Tries in Fiction: *Dawn* and *Witch's Head*

Dawn is a complicated intertangling of three stories, any one of which might have stood alone as a novel. The first story concerns the rivalry between cousins for the inheritance of the estates of Philip Caresfoot, Sr., a squire of ancient family, who is known throughout the countryside as ''Devil Caresfoot.'' He insists that his son, Philip, Jr., marry a wealthy childhood sweetheart. Instead, the young man secretly marries one of the girl's school friends who is the daughter of an impoverished German aristocrat. Philip, Jr.'s cousin George connives to reveal the marriage and to secure a consequent change of Philip, Sr's. will in his own favor. Philip, Jr., confronts his father in his study where the new will lies on the table. Wrongly believing that it has yet to be made official, Philip threatens the old man by withholding his heart medication. Father then drops dead.

The second story concerns Philip's schemes to regain his patrimony from evil George. The key to success appears to lie with his unloved daughter Angela, whose mother died in childhood. A creature of ethereal beauty and formidable scholarship, Angela loves a young Cambridge graduate, Arthur Heigham, but is pushed by her father toward marriage with George. Father allows Angela to become engaged to Arthur on condition that they spend a year apart without exchanging messages of any sort.

The third story begins when Arthur travels to Madeira. On board ship he meets fascinating Mildred Carr, a woman of the world who also happens to be the richest widow in England. Even after she learns of Arthur's engagement, she perseveres in a campaign of seduction. Meanwhile, back in England George is failing badly in his wooing of Angela. He resorts to a subterfuge, enlisting the help of a former mistress, Anne Bellamy, whom Haggard likens to an Egyptian sorceress, "the spirit of power." Anne goes to Madeira with her husband and drops in on Arthur. She persuades him to send Angela proof of continued devotion by returning a ring she gave him. Anne carries the ring back to Angela as proof that Arthur is dead. Now George pretends to be dying in order to trick Angela into a marriage which, she believes, will satisfy her father's wishes without endangering herself. Arthur, who has left Madeira to avoid further entangling himself with Mildred, arrives home the night of the wedding. Without waiting for explanations, he denounces Angela and throws George into a bramble bush, where he is killed by Arthur's dog. At the same time Anne's husband learns of her liaison with George. She attempts suicide by taking a vial of mysterious poison but succeeds only in paralyzing herself from the neck down. She begs forgiveness from Angela and offers to reveal the secrets of her black arts. Angela refuses the dangerous gift and goes into seclusion. Arthur runs back to Madeira and becomes Mildred's lover in the

physical sense. He begs her to marry him but she refuses, so long as
Angela stands in the way. At last Angela comes to reclaim Arthur,
and Mildred is left weeping before a statue of god Osiris in her
private museum of Egyptian antiquities.

It is not difficult to see why *Dawn* made no money. The profu-
sion of characters, the unlikely deaths, the intricate plot, and the
heavy reliance on coincidence to move the story along all over-
burden the novel. They obscure Haggard's aim of exploring problems of family life and physical passion within the confining bonds
of Victorian propriety. At the same time, it is easy to understand
why Cordy Jeaffreson and other serious critics encouraged Haggard
to go on writing fiction. The three powerful women who dominate
the story cannot be easily fitted into conventional Victorian molds.
Angela is more learned and Anne is more ruthless than any of the
men in the book. Mildred's unabashed pursuit of sensual pleasure
outside marriage is portrayed without censure. In addition, there
are eerie suggestions these these women lead strange secret lives,
Anne as a magician and Mildred in her room full of mummies.
Developing these ideas would require either a frank disavowal of
realism or a setting less constricting than rural Norfolk.

In his second novel Haggard simplified his plot and used his
South African experience to broaden possibilities for his characters.
Like *Dawn, The Witch's Head* begins with youngsters embroiled
in the matrimonial and property schemes of their elders. A ruthless
lawyer dedicates his life to ruining a grasping manufacturer who
long ago pushed his sweetheart into a disastrous marriage by pointing out the financial advantages the girl would reap for her debt-
ridden father, a boisterous rascally squire. Three orphans are
pawns in the lawyer's game: his nephew Ernest, and Dorothy and
Jeremy Jones, children of his old sweetheart who died a tragic early
death. Ernest becomes the boon companion of Jeremy who is
fiercely loyal, dim-witted, and distrustful of women. Plain, practical Dorothy is groomed by the lawyer for marriage to Ernest. This
plan is disrupted when the dazzling Ceswick sisters move into the
neighborhood. Florence is dark, intelligent, passionate, and
powerful. Eva is a fair, shining beauty without much common
sense. After a brief romance with Florence, Ernest falls for Eva and
they pledge eternal love. On a holiday cruise to the island of
Guernsey, Ernest encounters his licentious cousin Hugh in the
company of a pretty French girl. When the girl flirts with Ernest,
Hugh flies into a jealous rage and challenges him to a duel in

which Ernest fires the decisive shot.

To escape the clutches of the law, Ernest runs off to South Africa where he becomes the protégé of wise colonial administrators. Florence revenges herself on Ernest by talking Eva into a marriage with a nasty, low-born clergyman. When he gets the news, Ernest loses his bearings. "Eva's desertion struck his belief in womanhood to the ground and soon his religion lay in the dust beside it . . . . He took to evil ways. . . . . He raced horses, he went in with great success for love-affairs that he would have done better to leave alone. Sometimes . . . he drank—for the excitement of drinking, not for the love of it" (226). Ernest and Jeremy are saved from utter dissipation by the Zulu War, in which they fight heroically. They return to England. Jeremy becomes a farmer, Ernest a member of Parliament and later, governor of Australia. He marries Dorothy after all, despite a feeling that his ultimate destiny is bound up with Eva.

There are obvious autobiographical features in both *Dawn* and *Witch's Head*. The uneasy relationships between the heroes and the domineering old squires echo Haggard's ambiguous attitudes toward his father. The periods of atheism and amoral pleasure-seeking, which follow the heroes' disappointments in love correspond to Haggard's wild days in Pretoria. Real events and people from his South African experience are introduced in *Witch's Head*. Osborn and Shepstone are eulogized, Gladstone reviled. Ernest reenacts Haggard's narrow escape from an African ambush. These autobiographical elements do not, however, succeed in raising either novel to the level which Olive Schreiner achieved through the use of similar materials.

In the preface to the second edition of *African Farm* Schreiner put her finger on one important difference between her work and Haggard's. Some people, she noted, had assumed that the agnostic stranger met in the veld by young Waldo was the same person as the gentleman seducer of Lyndall. She denied it, insisting that real life was never so neat. People are apt to wander on and off the stage of one's existence without plan or purpose. Haggard will not stand for such aimless wanderings in his novels. He must stagemanage all entrances and exits, piling coincidence on coincidence until drama gives way to melodrama. His realism is consequently far from realistic, although his characters dress in current fashions, move in contemporary settings, and face believable difficulties. A second important difference between Schreiner's and Haggard's novels is that Schreiner does not draw people in black and white. She admits redeeming qualities in her unlovable characters. She allows defects in her hero and heroine. Lyndall engages attention precisely because she has lost her faith, her inhibitions, and her virginity. Haggard's heroes and heroines are often tempted to do likewise but draw back before the precipice. The women in particular are required to exemplify the highest ideals of spirituality and purity. This leaves his villains with heavy burdens to shoulder. Grasping lawyers cannot disclose the slightest trace of generosity. Jealous sisters must live only for the destruction of their rivals. Cads and bounders must work tirelessly at their schemes of vice.

Another difference between Haggard and Schreiner is to be found in their treatment of social class. The protagonists of *African Farm* are handicapped and mistreated in life partly because they lack the credentials of "ladies" and "gentlemen." The struggles of poor and obscure people are as important to Schreiner as the malaises of the rich. Haggard, on the other hand, reserves all his sympathy for the wellborn. He despises businessmen and manufacturers. Where they are not cast as villains, they are figures of fun, pilloried for their lapses of manners and taste. Dissenting clergy and lay preachers receive similar abuse. The good qualities of working-class people are emphasized only so long as they stay in their proper stations and render faithful service to their betters. All the heroes of Haggard's novels come from the landed class. Their families are ancient, their fathers are squires. His heroines are seldom rich but always connected to the upper middle class. Even when one of them is introduced as a barmaid, (Joan Haste) she is eventually revealed to be the daughter of a gentleman. "Breeding will out," in every case.

This narrowness of vision as much as anything else in his serious novels sets Haggard well apart from contemporaries such as Thomas Hardy who pursued some of the same objectives. Hardy's characters also struggle with problems of faith, fidelity, and love in a lonely universe ruled by chance. Hardy's romantic settings with their suggestions of lingering prehistoric and Roman influences recall Haggard's landscapes where living lovers embrace among the reminders and remains of the dead. Hardy certainly relies as much as Haggard on improbable coincidence to hurry his characters on toward predestined ends. But in Hardy's books everyone, not just the class of landed proprietors, confronts the deepest problems of the human condition. One will look in vain for an obscure Jude or milkmaid Tess in Haggard's realistic novels.

Finally, Haggard differs from more successful serious novelists of his day in his inability to keep preachy conservative politics out of his fiction. Readers of *Dawn* are forced to endure a ludicrous caricature of Liberalism in which a Cabinet minister explains that "the instinct of robbery is perhaps the strongest in human nature, and those who would rule humanity on its present basis must pander to it or fail. The party of progress means the party that can give the most spoil, taken from those that have, to those who have not. That is why Mr. Gladstone is such a truly great man; he understands better than anyone of his own age how to excite the greed of hungry voters and to guide it for his own ends" (223). Large sections of *The Witch's Head* rework in unconvincing fiction the lawyerlike case in favor of Shepstone's policies in South Africa which Haggard had so masterfully presented in *Cetywayo and His White Neighbours.*

Jess

As he grew more experienced Haggard somewhat softened these defects in his novels but never entirely eliminated them. Nor did he cease using them to relive vicariously the sufferings of his early disappointments in love. *Jess* transplants the contrasting sisters of *Witch's Head* into Schreiner's setting of a lonely African farm. The younger sister, Bessie, is beautiful but prosaic. The elder, Jess, is a feminist somewhat like Schreiner's Lyndall. "What was she to do with herself," she wonders, "Marry somebody and busy herself with rearing a pack of children? It would be a physical impossibility to her. No, she would go away to Europe and mix in the great stream of life and . . . win a place for herself among the people of her day. She had it in her, she knew that" (224). Unfortunately, Haggard does not give her the chance she seeks to prove herself. Instead she is caught up in a sticky love triangle. She and Bessie both desire a retired army officer John Niel who has come to farm ostriches with their father. In order to leave the field clear for her sister, Jess nobly renounces her claims and goes to live in Pretoria.

Bessie becomes engaged to John after spurning a proposal from a megalomaniac Boer nationalist, Frank Muller, who aspires to be president of an independent South Africa after the British are expelled. When the Transvaal rebellion breaks out, John goes to

Pretoria to rescue Jess. They are caught in the siege, virtually living together, although Jess bravely maintains her posture of renunciation. Muller plots to kill them so that he can have Bessie. They escape his clutches, only to be carried away by the raging torrent of a flash flood. Thinking they are about to die, they confess eternal love. Messy consequences might have ensued when they were saved but for the continuing scheming of mad Muller who has had the girls' father arrested on a charge of treason. He threatens that his Boer cronies will execute the old gentleman unless Bessie marries him. Jess averts the plot by murdering Muller in his sleep. She then runs raving into the bush where she eventually dies in a cave. John and Bessie marry and go to live in England where John finds work as an estate manager.

There are some fine moments in *Jess* which was deservedly the most financially successfully of Haggard's attempts at realism. It offers shrewd observations on the situation of South Africa's native peoples and perceptive comments on the Africanization of the frontier Boers. On the other hand, Haggard's portrayal of the motives and characters of the Transvaal leaders is unworthy of the author of *Cetywayo and his White Neighbours*. A Tory diatribe against "little Englandism" is put into the mouth of Paul Kruger who professes to despise the British for devotion to commerce. "It is all a question of shops, and if the shops abroad interfere with the shops at home, or if it is thought that they do, which comes to the same thing, then the shops at home put an end to the shops abroad." This and other unlikely speeches are enthusiastically seconded by the grotesque Frank Muller, who gratuitously adds that he "will destroy the natives, as T'Chaka destroyed, keeping only enough for slaves. That is my plan, uncle; it is a good one" (185-86). Such diversions, along with Haggard's monotonous harping on the subject of love versus fidelity, distract attention from the potentially interesting figure of Jess. A counterpart to Schreiner's portrayal of aspirant Victorian womanhood would have been a welcome addition to both Southern African and English literature.

Colonel Quaritch, V.C.

With *Colonel Quaritch, V.C.* (1888) Haggard retreated from that interesting terrain to the familiar ground of property squabbles among the declining English gentry. Squire de la Molle is beset on all sides by forces of the modern world which he is ill equipped to fight. Like "Devil Caresfoot" in *Dawn* and "Hard-riding Atterleigh" in *Witch's Head,* he is a caricature of Haggard's father. His devotion to queen, country, family honor, and the land do not suffice to keep him out of debt. The extravagances of his soldier son, the decline of English agriculture, and his bad business sense combine to place him in the clutches of lawyers and moneylenders. He hopes that his lovely daughter Ida will get him out of trouble by making a lucrative marriage. Her principal suitor is Edward Cossey, son of a London financier worth millions. He offers to cancel the old squire's mortgage provided that Ida becomes his wife. Though she is strongly attracted to the retired colonel who has just brought an adjoining property, she consents to be sold to save her father.

These plans are delayed by the intrigues of a local lawyer who nourishes a grievance against Cossey for seducing his wife. He threatens to name Cossey as correspondent in a divorce case, thus endangering his inheritance and ruining his marriage plans. Cossey gives in to the blackmail and assigns the mortgage to the lawyer, who then threatens to foreclose on de la Molle. This disaster is averted by one of the squire's faithful retainers who learns that the lawyer harbors a guilty secret of his own. As a teenager he had been tricked into marrying a London prostitute. Believing that the marriage was invalid, he subsequently married again only to learn to his horror that he was technically a bigamist. For years he paid blackmail to keep the old whore quiet. Now she threatens to tell all. They struggle in a railway carriage and fall to a gory death locked in each others' arms. The mortgage now reverts to Cossey who insists that Ida keep her promise. The day is saved by Colonel Quaritch who has deciphered an encoded clue to the burial place of an ancestral treasure of the de la Molles.

The chief virtue of *Quaritch, V.C.* is that it offers some really interesting characters in sordid situations paralleling the court cases in sensational newspapers to which Haggard had called attention in his article "About Fiction." The chief defect of the book is that those characters are all cast as sluts and rogues. The adulterous wife, the bigamist lawyer, the blackmailing prostitute, and the scampish financier are cardboard villains, always depicted in profile, never explored from the inside. Their intrigues are viewed at a safe distance from the perspective of the unsullied central characters. Colonel Quaritch is positively indifferent to sin and sex.

Over forty years of age, "he was not a marrying man, and women as a class had little attraction for him. . . . he had never married and never even had a love affair since he was five and twenty" (5). Ida is a bloodless, steadfastly dutiful daughter. Significantly, it is the disembodied purity of the image of her face that wins the colonel. It is inconceivable that either of these saintly, insipid lovers could be caught in the sort of romantic escapade which was endemic in the Haggard family and which Rider aspired to depict in his fiction.

Beatrice

Two years later, when he did finally dare to write about adultery from the inside, he got his fingers severely burned. The heroine of *Beatrice* (1890) has the brains and learning of Angela in *Dawn* combined with the ambition and atheism of Schreiner's Lyndall. At the age of seventeen, she spurns the proposal of an idle rich neighbor because "she did not covet wealth, she coveted independence, and had the sense to know that marriage with such a man would not bring it. . . . That a man with all this wealth and endless opportunity should waste his life in such fashion was to her a thing intolerable." She reads Darwin. She is a radical and a freethinker. "She knew that if she had half his chance, that she would make her name ring from one end of Europe to the other" (48). She acknowledges the truth of her sister's jibe that she is "a socialist about property" who wants "to pull everything down, from the Queen to the laws of marriage, all for the good of humanity" (78-79). However, like Jess before her, she is trapped in a life of sacrifice and unfulfilled love which stultifies all her ambitions. She falls in love with a married man, Geoffrey Bingham, who is a prominent barrister and a rising politician.

Haggard contrives their adulterous relationship with the utmost caution. Beatrice and Geoffrey are given good excuses for falling into each other's arms. She is being pushed by her venal father into a hateful but lucrative marriage; Geoffrey's wife is a cold, cynical, flirtatious social climber. Nevertheless, Haggard will not simply let nature take its course. He introduces the lovers in the dangerous circumstances of a coastal storm during which Beatrice saves Geoffrey from drowning. The life and death emergency, which produces an intimacy which propriety would otherwise prevent, was a device Haggard had used before in *Jess* and would use again in future novels. Even after the lovers have admitted their feelings and Beatrice has become the behind-the-scenes inspiration in Geoffrey's career, there is no physical intimacy. This comes much later when Beatrice walks in her sleep and wanders unintentionally into Bingham's bedroom. Her jealous sister Elizabeth sees everything and threatens to create a scandal. Beatrice fears a repetition of the Dilke case. "Oh, she saw it all—the great posters with her name and Geoffrey's on them, the shameless pictures of her in his arms, the sickening details, the letters of the outraged matrons, the 'Mothers of ten,' and the moral-minded colonels—all, all! She heard the prurient scream of every male Elizabeth in England; the allusions in the House—the jeers, the bitter attacks of enemies and rivals. Then Lady Honoria would begin her suit, and it would all be dragged up afresh, and Geoffrey's fault would be on every lip, till he was *ruined*" (251). There is only one way out. Beatrice commits suicide, ironically dying on the same day that Geoffrey's wife is accidentally killed in a fire.

Despite the melodramatic coincidences and the sleep walking scene *Beatrice* comes close to being the realistic novel Haggard recommended in "About Fiction." It portrays believable people in justifiable but socially unacceptable situations struggling to achieve a moral existence in a Darwinian world. It does this without resorting to the unblinking camera eye of the French naturalists and without any sort of eroticism. Beatrice is far more human, daring, and engaging than the spotless heroines of Haggard's earlier novels. All that separates her from Schreiner's Lyndall is her choice of duty and self-sacrifice in preference to feminism. A real-life feminist, Lady Florence Dixie, complained that Beatrice was "given no chance" and that the book proclaimed "the rooted idea in men's minds that women are born to suffer and work for men, to hide all their natural gifts that man may rule alone."

Heeding that criticism might have caused Haggard to direct the steps of future heroines along more adventurous paths. But he was oblivious to the attack from his left. What deeply concerned him was the objection from the right that *Beatrice* condoned immorality. It was reported that "an emotional lady, herself a Beatrice, found in this tale encouragement to indite a love-letter to her host a married man" and that "a clergyman of middle age, after perusing the history of its unfortunate heroine, disturbed the peace of his household by paying attention to some person who was not his wife.'' Haggard wrote an indignant disclaimer in the next edition, saying that he had ''never dreamed that his study of an ill-disciplined but beautiful character could be chosen as a text for wrong, even by the most inexperienced or the most unclean.'' He pointed readers to his moral that ''whatever the excuse or tempta-tion, the man or woman who falls into undesirable relations with a married member of the other sex is both a sinner and a fool, and, in this coin or that, certainly will be called upon to pay the price of sin and folly'' (''Advertisement'' to the second edition). He deter-mined not to let his future heroines go so far astray. He put on again his mask of tory squire which had evidently slipped too far for his personal comfort.

Later Novels

Joan Haste (1895) told a potentially more daring story in such a way as to render it quite safe. At the center of the tale is the tragedy of an unmarried mother but there are no feminists, freethinkers or somnambulating adulterers among the central characters. A disgraced gentleman of ancient family lives under the pseudonym of Levinger in a quiet coastal town, haunted by the consequences of bigamy. Like the scheming lawyer of *Colonel Quaritch*, his first marriage was a disastrous misalliance with a lowborn tart. Thinking her dead, he married again—for money—only to be eventually confronted by his errant original wife and infant daughter. The mother conveniently jumps off a cliff but the daughter lives on to be raised by the local publican's wife, with surreptitious support from her father. The daughter of the second marriage is educated as a lady and aspires to marry the dashing naval officer Henry Graves, second son of the local lord of the manor. Henry comes within her reach when his wastrel older brother dies, leaving the family groaning under an impossible load of debt. Though Henry hates giving up his naval career and has never cared much for women, he is attracted by the ''spirituality'' of Emma Levinger and therefore inclined to go along with his parents' desire that he marry the heiress. However, an accidental fall lays him up for weeks at the local tavern where Levinger's unacknowledged daughter Joan nurses him back to health. The in-timacy that grows up while Henry is in danger of dying leads to a few minutes of passionate physical contact.

The affair is prevented from developing by Henry's dying

father, who demands that Henry marry Emma. Joan disappears, partly to get Henry off the hook and partly to escape the proposals of a lunatic farmer. She finds work in London as a model and then discovers that she is pregnant. In the midst of a sick delirium, she writes a letter to Henry which her landlady finds and mails. Henry promises marriage but before he can get to London his mother visits Joan and asks that she sacrifice her own interests to save an ancient family. At this point the crazy farmer Samuel Rock arrives. Joan agrees to marry him on condition that they live apart for a year. Henry, thinking that Joan is a slut, forgets her and marries Emma. A year later, after the death of her baby, Joan returns to the little town, learns the truth about her parentage, and sets out to see her loathsome husband. On the way, she meets Henry by chance. They make their mutual explanations and fall into a tearful embrace. Unfortunately, they are observed by Joan's husband, who subsequently locks her up, picks up his rifle, and goes hunting for Henry. Joan dresses herself in man's clothing, escapes from the house, and walks deliberately into her husband's ambush.

In the hands of another author, Theodore Dreiser for example, *Joan Haste* might have been an engrossing story of seduction across class lines, complicated by ambition for money and respectability. Haggard will not permit that. By making Joan half a lady by birth and allowing her a brief boarding school education, he blurs class distinctions. By making Henry steadfastly determined to do the decent and honorable thing, he avoids facing up to the complex countertugs of physical desire and social pressure that would have torn any believable English gentleman in Henry's position. The novel thus becomes just another melodrama of love among the squirearchy, with all the heroes recruited from the upper middle class and all the scoundrels drawn from the lower orders. Repulsive Samuel Rock is a dissenter in religion whose weekday rantings on his farm are echoes of Sunday rantings in the chapel. The publican and his wife injure Joan with their venality; the London landlady injures Joan with her ignorance. And, of course, coincidences abound.

After *Joan Haste* Haggard wrote only five more "novels," though his output of "romances" remained steady. The later novels moved farther away from the high point reached in *Beatrice.* They are increasingly preoccupied with reincarnation as a means of explaining why men so often marry the wrong women. The answer is that in the hereafter or in subsequent incarnations true lovers will conquer the barriers thrown up in this life by class, chance, and social pressure. *Stella Fregelius* (1904) begins in the world of Jules Verne's science fiction and ends in the realms of Madame Blavatsky's theosophy. Morris Monk of Monk's Abbey is an inventor approaching middle age. He is trying to invent a wireless telephone, much to the disgust of his father, a debt-ridden roué who hopes to marry him off to his wealthy cousin Mary. Morris, who is largely indifferent to women, agrees to become engaged. Before the marriage can take place, Morris and Mary are separated for several months because of her father's illness. A Danish ship runs aground in a gale near Monk's Abbey and Morris effects a daring rescue of Stella Fregelius. The two are swept out to sea in Morris's little sailboat and get to know each other well during their hours of mortal danger.

Love ripens in the months to come, as Stella helps Morris to perfect his "aerophone." Stella expounds her religious beliefs, which are a weird compound of Viking paganism and orthodox Christianity. When Stella refuses an offer of marriage from the son of a wealthy manufacturer, rumors spread that her relationship with Morris is less than Platonic. She decides to renounce her love and make her living as a musician in London. After tearful good-byes, Morris and Stella stage a "spiritual marriage" in the seaside ruined church which they had previously used for aerophone experiments. Stella lingers behind, falls asleep, and awakes in the midst of a storm that is breaking down the sea cliff around the church. She makes one last phone call to Morris and then dies singing an ancient Viking dirge. Morris marries his cousin, becomes rich and famous, but cannot forget his lost love. He begins experiments in communication with the dead and gradually comes to prefer their company. In a final mystical meditation he fasts himself into the hereafter.

Like the earlier novels, *Stella* is an exercise in veiled autobiography. There again is the eccentric squire getting in the way of his son's marriage plans. There again is the abiding sense of brooding death: "Life is a queer game of blind man's buff, isn't it; played in a mist on a mountain top, and the players keep dropping over the precipices. But nobody heeds, because there are always plenty more, and the game goes on forever" (37). There, also, are the venal clergymen, the contemptible nouveaux riches, the prosaic wife. However, the problems of love and desire which most deeply troubled Haggard in his own life are more than ever held at arm's length. Morris Monk resembles Captain Neil, Colonel Quaritch, and Captain Graves in his miraculous immunity to physical desire before the age of thirty. In this respect he is quite unlike Haggard and his scapegrace brothers. The exaggerated emphasis on the utter purity of Morris's love for Stella evades the sexual issue. The tediously prolonged discourses on love after death similarly evade the issue of Christianity versus atheism and paganism.

It is not surprising that Haggard wrote few "novels" in later years. *Stella* reeks too much of the supernatural to be seriously considered as realist. More important, the "novel" had simply not proved to be an effective medium of self-expression for a reticent Tory gentleman. Haggard's habitual respect for propriety prevented him from allowing further experiments in faith and morals along the lines of *Beatrice*. Escape into the hereafter provided a false resolution of the doubts and guilts which afflicted him along with so many educated people of his generation. It was not because he lacked skill or imagination that he failed to emulate the achievements of Olive Schreiner. It was because he lacked nerve. What he could do when he felt safe was amply demonstrated by his success in following the way suggested by Robert Louis Stevenson in *Dr. Jekyll and Mr. Hyde*.

Chapter Three
The Early Romances
Haggard, *Dr. Jekyll* and Dr. Freud

Dr. Jekyll and Mr. Hyde had an electrifying effect on Haggard. In places, he wrote, the horror of it was "enough to cause the hair to rise."[1] Its arresting theme was the duality of man. A high-principled scientist develops a formula which turns him into a dissolute monster. As Dr. Jekyll, he exemplifies the highest type of civilized man. As Mr. Hyde, he revels in vice, and kills without remorse. Dr. Jekyll explains all this in scientific terms. He has discovered "that man is not truly one but truly two."[2] The drug, by shaking "the very fortress of identity," revealed a distinct personality which had always lurked within him. He suspects that future scientists will discover more personalities and that man will ultimately be shown to be "a mere polity of multifarious incongruous and independent denizens." This revelation is frightening because although Dr. Jekyll recognizes the evil of Hyde, he secretly longs to be him. At the moment of transition he is conscious of "a current of disordered sensual images running like a mill race in my fancy, a solution of the bonds of obligation, an unknown but not an innocent freedom of the soul." To put it simply, Hyde lacks a Victorian conscience. He has no repressed desires because he does not know the meaning of repression.

Well might Rider Haggard shiver with horror at the story of Jekyll and Hyde. He, who was so fearful of revealing his secret thoughts and desires that he felt that if they were ever committed to paper, the incriminating manuscript must be buried for at least five hundred years, felt a palpable shudder at the prospect of the beast within himself being released to roam at large in England.[3] And he also felt the attraction of such a release, just as he had felt the attraction of life among the Zulus who appeared to lack so many of the stifling restraints of Victorian society.

At the base of *Jekyll and Hyde* is a very old idea. Ancient Greek philosophers expressed it as a distinction between spirit and matter. The founders of the Christian Church dramatized it as the struggle of the individual soul to free itself from the evil appetites of the body and to attain salvation as pure spirit. The idea cropped up again among the European romantics who personified the savage side of man sometimes as noble and sometimes as darkly evil.[4] On the other hand, there is something distinctly novel about Stevenson's presentation of this old idea. He expresses it, not in terms of abstract philosophy or religion, not as a metaphor, but as a hard scientific fact. His conception had direct parallels among real men of science in his own day. In the twilight of the Victorian era new psychological models were emerging which conceptualized the self as a series of conscious and unconscious layers. Already Sigmund Freud in Vienna was well along the path which would lead him to roll together vague conceptions of the subconscious into a coherent theory of the psyche which he, like Jekyll, took to be proven fact. "The fortress of identity" was shaken indeed.

It is the thesis of this chapter that Haggard's early romances expounded and dramatized a theory of the psyche that bore a close resemblance to Freud's conception. Haggard shuddered at *Jekyll and Hyde* because he believed himself to possess a similarly divided personality. The late-Victorian readers who shuddered with him flocked to buy his own romances because they consciously or unconsciously recognized them as embodying the same fascinating, threatening concept. Support for this proposition can be found both among later novelists who have admired Haggard's work and among the progenitors of psychoanalysis.

Henry Miller has expressed his fascination with the contrast between the conventional, public face of Haggard the public figure, and the fantastic, unconventional world of imagination revealed in his romances:

There is a duality in Rider Haggard which intrigues me enormously. An earthbound individual, conventional in his ways, orthodox in his beliefs . . . this man who is reticent and reserved, English to the core, one might say, reveals through his "romances" a hidden nature, a hidden being, a hidden lore which is amazing. His method of writing these romances—at full speed, hardly stopping to think, so to speak—enabled him to tap his unconscious with freedom and depth.[5]

Graham Greene likewise praises Haggard for conveying in a direct and vital way the central problems of identity and duality in the human personality: "There are thousands of names for it, King Solomon's Mines, the 'heart of darkness' if one is romantically inclined, or more simply, as Herr Heuser puts it in his African novel 'The Inner Journey,' one's place in time, based on a knowledge not only of one's present but of the past from which one has emerged.''[6] Margaret Atwood sees exactly the same link between Haggard and Joseph Conrad: ''the journey into the unknown regions of the self, the unconscious, and the confrontation with whatever dangers and splendors lurk there.''[7]

The founders of psychoanalysis, Sigmund Freud and C. G. Jung, also took Haggard's romances very seriously. Some time between 1897 and September 1899 Freud, the celebrated interpreter of dreams, actually dreamed about two of Haggard's novels. This was Freud's dream: he found himself in the laboratory engaged in the gruesome work of dissecting his own pelvis and legs. The scene then changed to a perilous journey through a wild landscape peopled by savages (''Red Indians or gipsies''). At the end of the journey he had to cross a chasm on narrow planks. He awoke in a ''mental fright.''[8] Despite the rich sexual imagery of the dream, Freud's interpretation stressed its intellectual content. Self-dissection he identified with his daring and traumatic self-analysis which was in progress at the time. The Indians came from Haggard's *Heart of the World* (1895) and the wild landscape from *She* (1887). Both books were on Freud's mind because of a recent conversation with a patient:

"Lend me something to read," she said. I offered her Rider Haggard's *She*. "A strange book, but full of hidden meaning," and began to explain to her: "the eternal feminine, the immortality of our emotions. . . . ." Here she interrupted me: "I know it already. Have you nothing of your own?"—"No, my own immortal works have not yet been written." "Well, when are we to expect these so-called ultimate explanations of yours which you've promised even we shall find readable?" she asked, with a touch of sarcasm.

The production of his own ''immortal works'' suggested to Freud the content of *She* which ''describes an adventurous road that had scarcely ever been trodden before, leading into an undiscovered region.'' At the same time Freud feared that the fate of Haggard's heroine might be his own—that death rather than immortality waited at the end of the adventure.

Freud and Jung, it can be argued, took a particular interest in Haggard because they saw in his novels an implicit model of the self which corresponded closely to their own explicit models.

King Solomon's Mines

Consider, for example, *King Solomon's Mines* (1885), the first and still the most widely read of the romances. The book quite deliberately attempted to repeat the success of Robert Louis Stevenson's *Treasure Island* (1883). Written in six weeks, it was Haggard at his most automatic, fusing a highly imaginative narrative from bits and pieces of legends and stories which he had collected during the five years he spent in South Africa. The book is often cited as a typical example of "imperialism in literature." This is an odd view to take, because Haggard went out of his way to avoid drawing on his personal involvement with colonialism in Africa. He could, for example, easily have turned to his experience as a private secretary to Governor Bulwer of Natal, aide to Sir Theophilus Shepstone during the annexation of the Transvaal, and partner in an ostrich farming venture. Instead, he cast his eyes north to parts of the African interior which were just beginning to be opened up to European eyes.

The recently discovered stone ruins at Great Zimbabwe almost certainly provided the inspiration for the ruined mines of King Solomon. Haggard would have known of them from the picture of the ruins which appears at one corner of J. R. Jeppe's "Map of the Transvaal Republic," published in the same year as Shepstone's annexation. Ancient gold diggings were known to exist in many parts of the Zimbabwe plateau and were picturesquely identified by Thomas Baines's "Map of the Gold Fields of South Eastern Africa" (1873) as the "Supposed Realm of Queen of Sheba." Other elements in Haggard's story may well have been borrowed from a forgotten novel by Hugh Mulleneux Walmsley published in 1869 as *The Ruined Cities of Zululand* and reissued ten years later under the title *Wild Sports and Savage Life in Zululand.* Walmsley was the son of Joshua Walmsley, M.P., and the brother of the Natal border agent who served as Shepstone's eyes and ears on the Zulu frontier. Quite apart from its suggestive title, Walmsley's book contains several incidents which figure prominently in Haggard's first romance. After a series of dangerous hunting adventures, Walmsley's heroes encounter a German missionary named Wyzinski who has devoted much of his life to a quest for Ophir and the wrecked ships of Pharaoh Necho. Walmsley's novel also includes an encounter with Amatonga who divide into warring factions when a good native accuses the wicked and hideously ugly chief of misrule. The chief's wife is an ancient, vengeful hag.

We have Haggard's own testimony that the "Kukuana" people of *King Solomon's Mines* were modeled on the Matabele (Ndebele) people of Zimbabwe. In the late 1860s, a man who had once worked as a gardener for Theophilus Shepstone in Natal proclaimed himself the rightful heir to the Matabele kingship held by Lobengula. A party of gold-seekers consisting of Sir John Swinburne, Captain A. L. Levert, and the old South African explorer Thomas Baines flirted briefly with the idea of upholding this claim in order to win a mining concession. Haggard cunningly grafted these elements of fact and fiction onto Stevenson's device of the treasure map to produce a compelling story whose essential elements were to be reproduced in most of the later romances.[9]

A party of three whites—a wise old hunter, a handsome young aristocrat, and an excessively English naval officer—set off in search of the nobleman's lost brother and fabled diamond mines sketched on a faded Portuguese parchment. They are accompanied by a highly intelligent, haughty, and superbly muscled African. The party slaughters cartloads of big game, crosses a scorching desert, and passes along narrow defiles through spectacular mountain scenery until Kukuana-land sparkles gemlike before their feet. There the adventurers find a Zulu-speaking people whose neat, hygienic villages dot the countryside of a pastoral Elysium. Amid stone ruins testifying to the glories of a vanished civilization, a tyrannical king rules the Kukuanas with the aid of his cruel son and a centuries-old shriveled hag. At a savage ceremony the whites intervene to prevent the sacrifice of a beautiful maiden, thereby enraging the king and his retainers. Now the mysterious African who accompanied the whites reveals himself as the rightful king of the land and gathers supporters to challenge the tyrant. Thousands die in the ensuing battle in which the white men distinguish themselves in the service of their former guide. The victorious new king rewards his friends by forcing the old witch to lead them to a secret treasure cave where the diamonds are stored. While trapping the white party in the cave, the witch is herself killed by the beautiful maiden who has won the love of the naval officer. The party manages an escape through subterranean caverns, minus the maiden, and carries off enough diamonds to make the whole trip worthwhile. After the whites refuse an offer to make them lords in the land, the king announces his intention to seal off Kukuanaland against any future European incursions. The whites make their way back to England, happily saving the aristocrat's long-lost brother on the way.

Certainly there are elements of classical imperialism in this scenario. Big game and diamonds conjure up visions of boundless African wealth; the attribution of the ruins to vanished whites discounts African ability; the tyranny of the bad king is a caricature of savagery; and the death of the maiden conveniently removes the threat of miscegenation. Much more remarkable, however, are the features which do not accord with stereotypes of Victorian imperialism. The rightful king is no shuffling clown but a proud and intelligent aristocrat who will not conform to the subservient role which the old hunter Quatermain insists that he play. Daily life in Kukuanaland is healthy, tidy, and chaste—soap, civilization, and missionaries are not wanted here. There is a real interracial love story, not mere concubinage; the naval officer swears after his return to Europe that no Englishwoman could hold a candle to the lost Foulata "either as regards her figure or the sweetness of her expression."[10] The book ends on a strongly anti-imperialist note as the Kukuana king vows to keep Europeans out of his domain: "No other white man shall cross the mountains. . . . I will see no traders with their guns and gin. . . . I will have no praying-men to put a fear of death into men's hearts, to stir them up against the law of the king, and make a path for the White folk who follow to run on" (205). As imperialist indoctrination this is distinctly weak.[11]

Taking up Atwood's suggestion that the trek into Africa is a trek from the known into the unconscious unknown self, a different message emerges from the events of the novel. Haggard's whites are all stock European types: hunter Allan Quatermain is a grizzled old colonial with colonial prejudices; Sir Henry Curtis is a gentleman of no African experience but willing to learn and inclined to treat Africans as equals; Captain Good of the Royal Navy is comically dedicated to maintaining English dress and manners regardless of climate or latitude. These three representatives of civilization undergo a series of punishing tests. The tests are progressively severe and are marked by changes of terrain. First the party is tested in a straight contest with big game in which Good narrowly escapes being trampled by an elephant because of his "passion for civilized dress," but he and the others prove themselves as brave sportsmen. Tests of desert heat, mountain cold, and starvation follow. But the greatest tests are moral and take place in the special secluded landscape of Kukuanaland. The trio are confronted in rapid succession by a slaughter of accused witches (likened by Haggard to a Roman gladiatorial show and the execution of the nobility in revolutionary

France), an orgiastic dance in which ravishingly beautiful women "pirouette . . . with a grace and vigour which would have put most ballet girls to shame," and an offer of free girls for the duration of their stay.

Next there is an extraordinary trial by battle, a feature of which is the savagery of the whites and the civilization of the blacks. Ignosi, the rightful king, is compared to a Roman emperor in charge of magnificently disciplined regiments. His order that no enemy wounded should be killed is obeyed without exception. "Never before," remarks Quatermain, "had I ever seen such an absolute devotion to the idea of duty." The three white men, on the other hand, all succumb to homicidal mania. Good longs for a Gatling gun with which to mow down the enemy. Quatermain, who previously professed an utter loathing for war, finds that in the heat of battle his blood, hitherto "half frozen with horror," pounds through his veins and he is possessed by "a savage desire to kill and spare not" (148). Even more spectacular is the conversion of Sir Henry Curtis who goes out to fight clad in leopard skins and ostrich feathers—a replica of Ignosi. At the climax of the struggle, his Viking ancestry asserts itself and he kills for the sheer joy of killing:

There he stood, the great Dane, for he was nothing else, his hands, his axe, and his armour all red with blood, and none could live before his stroke. Time after time I saw it sweeping down, as some great warrior ventured to give him battle, and as he struck he shouted "O-hoy! O-hoy!" like his Berserker forefathers, and the blow went crashing through shield and spear, through head dress, hair and skull. (150)

The last of Haggard's tests points up the moral challenges that preceded it. Gripped by mortal terror, the heroes listen as the ancient witch Gagool cackles materialistic philosophy at them:

"The old feel not, they love not, and, ha! ha! they laugh to see another go out into the dark; ha! ha! they laugh to see the evil that is done under the stars. All they love is life, the warm, warm sun, and the sweet, sweet air. They are afraid of the cold, afraid of the cold and the dark, ha! ha! ha!" and the old hag writhed in ghastly merriment on the ground. (167)

Haggard's characters have moved progressively through a symbolic landscape from physical tests to moral tests. The closer the adventurers come to the mines, the farther they are removed from the psychological and moral verities of their age. The severity of the tests is underlined by Sir Henry Curtis in a speech made just before the final push into Kukuanaland. "Gentlemen . . . we are going on about as strange a journey as men can make in this world." Strong images reinforce the message that the way to *King Solomon's Mines* lies beyond the frontiers of Victorian taboos. To reach the hidden valley it is necessary to pass over the mountains called "Sheba's Breasts": "Let him who comes follow the map, and climb the snow of Sheba's left breast till he reaches the nipple; on the north side of which is the great road Solomon made" (23). The ruins near the . . . . . . are "sculptured with rude emblems of the Phallic worship."

There are also strong suggestions that the real aim of the search is to rediscover or uncover lost aspects of oneself. Curtis is looking for his lost brother, that is, his own image. Two hidden aspects of the self are dramatically revealed in Kukuanaland. One is a black, uncivilized self. The other is an ancient self. Ignosi is the uncivilized self. Haggard goes out of his way to stress the likeness between the black African king and the white English knight: " ' They make a good pair, don't they?' said Good; 'one as big as the other' " (30). When Curtis puts on his leopard skins, Ignosi immediately appears "arrayed in a similar costume," Allan Quatermain remarks that he "had never before seen two such splendid men." The ancient self uncovered in Kukuanaland is identified with previous "stages" in the development of European civilization. The setting is Egyptian or Phoenician. Ignosi chants in "a language as beautiful and sonorous as the old Greek." Curtis in battle is simultaneously the image of a black warrior king and a medieval Viking. The savage self and the ancient self are closely related and yet not identical. Haggard thus goes well beyond Stevenson's *Jekyll and Hyde* in his delineation of alternative personalities hidden beneath the surface of Victorian propriety. The individual psyche has indeed become what Jekyll suspected it might be: "a mere polity of multifarious and independent denizens."

Exploring these alternative identities is fun at first. Captain Good ceases to insist on civilized dress and goes about with a half-shaved beard. Curtis is bedazzled by his own beauty when he gets into his leopard skins. Even the incredible immersion in gore and slaughter which takes place in the climactic battle scene is exhilarating. But ultimately it is frightening to peel away layer after layer of oneself, each time finding a new personality with its own laws and mores, each of which is more wild than the previous one. At the mines themselves Gagool is there to drive home the point. All is flux and matter.

Nature is red in tooth and claw. There is no God and no moral law.[12] The heart of Africa is in *King Solomon's Mines* just what Conrad said it was in *Heart of Darkness*—a special psychological terrain in which European man confronts and nearly succumbs to his deepest fears. This exotic world is infinitely more interesting than the world depicted in Haggard's "realistic" novels. It is largely free from his peculiar private obsessions about property and disappointments in love. It presents in many guises and variations the obsessions Haggard shared with his Victorian readers: the fearful recognition of subconscious alter egos, the fragility of "civilization," the relativity of morality in a post-Darwinian universe.

Allan Quatermain and *She*

Haggard rearranged and developed these themes in his next two romances. *Allan Quatermain* (1887) is another quest, this time for a lost white civilization rumored to exist in the center of the African continent. The white trio of *King Solomon's Mines* is resuscitated and reinforced by Umslopogaas, the bravest Zulu of them all. Haggard prepares his audience with a soliloquy on civilization and savagery. Quatermain has tired of prissy England and longs to go back to Africa "where the wild game was, back to the land whereof none know the history, back to the savages, whom I love, although some of them are almost as merciless as Political Economy."[13] He goes on to make explicit the sociology and psychology which was implicit in *King Solomon's Mines:*

Ah! this civilization, what does it all come to? . . . . It is a depressing conclusion, but in all essentials the savage and the child of civilization are identical. I dare say that the highly civilized lady reading this will smile at an old fool of a hunter's simplicity when she thinks of her black bead-bedecked sister. . . . And yet, my dear young lady, what are those pretty things round your own neck. . . ?
This being so, supposing for the sake of argument we divide ourselves into twenty parts, nineteen savage and one civilized, we must look to the nineteen savage portions of our nature, if we would really understand ourselves, and not to the twentieth, which, though so insignificant in reality, is spread all over the other nineteen, making them appear quite different from what they really are, as the blacking does a boot, or the veneer a table. (4-6)

Haggard illustrates his theory by once again moving a white party through a progressively bizarre series of landscapes in which physical stamina and moral fiber are tested to the limits of endurance. Man hunting supersedes big game hunting very early when the heroic quartet, augmented by a preternaturally ferocious missionary, lays siege to a Masai encampment. The heroes snap necks "like dry twigs" and unleash a murderous barrage of rifle fire. Sir Henry Curtis and Umslopogaas finish side by side swinging battle-axes with deadly effect until both are "red from head to foot—Sir Henry's armor might have been painted that color," and the dead lie strewn about "for all the world like the people on the grass in one of the London parks on a particularly hot Sunday in August". (86)

After the fight, the party moves on through a subterranean river and a prodigious chasm to reach the lost white "civilization." Zu-Vendis, as the country is called, is a blend of Kukuanaland and feudal England. The inhabitants have no technology other than architecture and are for the most part peasant farmers. An aristocracy somewhat lighter in color than the common people rules the land in conjunction with a superstitious and jesuitical priesthood. This setting gives Haggard another opportunity to make the point that our ancestral past lurks just a little way beneath the surface of our contemporary identities. Even before reaching Zu-Vendis, the heroes have put on chain mail armor. Once inside the kingdom, they enter into a world of chivalry and courtly love. (Haggard, with his distrust of bourgeois values, cannot forbear making observations about the superiority of this agriculture-based society to modern England. His portrait of Zu-Vendis feudalism prefigures his own later work as an agricultural reformer.) His heroes side firmly with the state in its conflict with a corrupt church. At the same time, Haggard gives the Zu-Vendis people a sexual freedom unknown in feudal England. In daily life the Zu-Vendis people are polygamous and inclined toward libertinism. A quarrel between sister queens over the love of Sir Henry Curtis precipitates a civil war which very nearly surpasses the sanguinary climax of *King Solomon's Mines*. At the end of the book Sir Henry elects to remain in Zu-Vendis to guard the kingdom against outside penetration:

I am convinced of the sacred duty that rests upon me of preserving to this, on the whole, upright and generous-hearted people the blessings of comparative barbarism. . . . I have no fancy for handing over this beautiful country to be torn and fought for by speculators, tourists, politicians and teachers . . . nor will I endow it with the greed, drunkenness, new diseases, gunpowder, and general demoralization which chiefly mark the progress of civilization amongst unsophisticated peoples. (276-77)

At this stage the parallel with *King Solomon's Mines* is so close that one wonders why Haggard painted the Zu-Vendis white and the Kukuanas black. In life-style and outlook they are nearly identical. Haggard even has his heroes use their Zulu titles among the Zu-Vendis. "Are the Zu-Vendi a civilized or a barbarous people?" Quatermain asks himself; "Sometimes I think the one, sometimes the other" (156). The real point of bringing color and ancient ruins into the romance is not to make statements about race but to make statements about us, about our psychology, our past. In Zu-Vendis, as in the Kukuanaland of *King Solomon's Mines,* white men discover their own interior savage selves—Sir Henry Curtis puts on skins and feathers, and becomes an African; he picks up a battle-ax and becomes a Viking; he puts on chain-mail and becomes a medieval knight. Ruins of vanished white civilizations remind us that the Africa that is our deepest self—the nineteen savage parts—is also our past. The real Africa which Haggard knew well, the Africa of disease, squalor, and stinking corruption, was the last thing he wished to put into his romances. As a result, he could not write into his stories the brand of racism he casually espoused. His purpose was to use Africans to lay bare the inner core of European man, and he had, therefore, to emphasize similarities rather than differences.

In *She* (1887), Haggard exaggerated two minor features of *King Solomon's Mines*: challenges to Victorian sexual conventions and speeches on behalf of Nietzschean morality. A two-thousand-year-old Persian priestess waits for the reincarnation of her ancient lover in the heart of Africa where she rules a savage people among the ruins of a vanished race. The reincarnated lover, Cambridge-educated and accompanied by a grizzled don, makes his way toward his destiny with the aid of an inscribed potsherd. (In this story the identification of present European man with an African past is made explicit.) Along the way the travelers encounter not only the usual big animals and gruesome fights, but also a wide range of perversions and inversions of conventional mores. She's people are handsome but sullen cannibals of indeterminate race ("whitish-yellow"). Local custom makes women the aggressors in sexual affairs. Marriages are sealed with a kiss and as easily dissolved. The wisest old man of the cannibals is a self-confessed necrophiliac who as a boy fell in love with one of the ancient mummies that litter the landscape:

I learned to love that dead form. . . . I would creep up to her and kiss her cold face, and wor.der . . . who had loved and embraced her in the days that long had passed away . . . till one day my mother . . . followed me, and . . . half in dread, and half in anger . . . set fire to her hair, and she burnt fiercely, even down to the feet. . . . Presently his face brightened, and with an exclamation he pulled something forth . . . and revealed to my astonished gaze a beautifully shaped and almost white woman's foot, looking as fresh and firm as though it had but now been placed there.[14]

Other flaming mummies illuminate nocturnal orgies. More than one man in the story tends to misogyny and flies into a jealous rage when a woman competes for the attention of his beloved male companion.

Presiding over the whole carnival of perversions is Ayesha (She), the masterwork of Haggard's imagination. In many ways Ayesha is Gagool from *King Solomon's Mines* tarted up to be sexually devastating, a Diana in jack-boots who preaches materialism in philosophy and fascism in politics. Social Darwinism enables her to pursue her ends without regard to her means:

Those who are weak must perish; the earth is to the strong, and the fruits thereof. For every tree that grows a score shall wither, that the strong one may take their share. We run to place and power over the dead bodies of those who fail and fall; ay, we win the food we eat from out the mouths of starving babes. It is the scheme of things.'' (215)

She amuses herself with chemistry and eugenics (her servants are specially bred deaf mutes and she boasts of having once ''reared a race of giants'').[15] Her favorite ruling techniques are terror and torture. She despises democracy and hates Jews. She proposes to go off to England, overthrow Victoria, and reign in tandem with her lover: ''In the end she would, I had little doubt, assume absolute rule over the British dominions, and probably over the whole earth, and, though I was sure that she would speedily make ours the most glorious and prosperous empire that the world has ever seen, it would be at the cost of a terrible sacrifice of life''. (264)

Here is imperialism in reverse—England to be invaded by an irresistible African conqueror. Haggard's heroes succumb totally to this onslaught. In a striking scene, Leo Vincey is confronted with his own image in the mummified figure of his ancient self, Kallikrates the Greek. Realizing his destiny, he forgets Victorian morality and allows himself to be seduced over the corpse of a former lover. The Cambridge don throws himself shamelessly at Ayesha's feet. Only an accident saves the British throne. When Ayesha proposes to confer immortality on Leo by immersing him in fire deep within a fathomless cavern, he is at first reluctant. Ayesha tries to allay his fears by dancing stark naked into the fire, as she had done once thousands of years before. This time something goes wrong and she ages two thousand years in a few terrifying moments. It was the most unforgettable scene Haggard ever wrote.

Cleopatra and *The World's Desire*

The basic themes and characters which were developed in Haggard's first three romances continued to dominate his writing until about 1895. This was the most fruitful period of his career as a writer of fiction. He himself believed that his best work as a writer of romance was done in the period between the publication of *King Solomon's Mines* (1885) and *Montezuma's Daughter* (1893).[16] *Allan's Wife* (1889) takes hunter Quatermain to yet another unknown country dotted with ruins; there he is pitted in mortal combat against a white baboon lady who hates him for having won the love of her mistress: "I am a woman as she is, and you are a man, and they say in the kraals that men love women better than women love women. But it is a lie."[17] *Cleopatra* (1889) and *The World's Desire* (1890) replayed the theme of beautiful, power-hungry women capable of seducing all men and subverting all established values. Haggard's keen interest in ancient Greece and Egypt would naturally have suggested Cleopatra and Helen of Troy as subjects after the immense success of *She*. Cleopatra emerges in Haggard's treatment more as a dedicated enemy of family life and woman's subordination to man than as an Egyptian patriot. Marriage she denounces as "the iron link of enforced, unchanging union" which constitutes "the worst slavery of our sex, which, by the selfish will of man, the stronger, still binds us to a bed grown hateful, and enforces a service that love mayhap no longer hallows" (205-6). *Cleopatra* also develops another of Haggard's important themes to a greater extent than any of the other early novels. That is the notion that each person carries, in the buried chambers of the subconscious, memories of the evolution of life on earth. The hero of the novel sees dream pictures (as Haggard later claimed to see himself). In one he sees "the world as it had been before man was" when "monstrous brutes plunged and wallowed" in the seas. In another he sees "man as he was tens of thousands of years ago," when he had "the nature of the ape more than the nature of mankind'' (58). This notion that modern "civilized" people harbor within themselves elements of previous stages of evolution deepens his development of the Jekyll and Hyde metaphor. It gives the primitive, violent, animalistic side of man a time dimension. It presents in literature the then fashionable biological theory of recapitulation which posits that an animal in the early stages of growth "recapitulates" the evolution undergone by its ancestors in previous ages.[18]

Eric Brighteyes and *Nada the Lily*

Both the idea of the hidden, savage self and the idea of recapitulation are expounded in different ways in *Eric Brighteyes* (1891) and *Nada the Lily* (1892). They make an instructive pair of novels inasmuch as one cast of characters is all white and Viking while the other is entirely black and Zulu. Except for skin color, however, the books are almost interchangeable. A hero is raised from infancy in the company of the woman he loves; there is more than a hint of incest. Umslopagaas grows up believing Nada to be his sister. Eric plays as a child both with the lovely Gudruda and the witchlike Swanhild, who are themselves half-sisters. A rejecting father figure then casts out the hero who is forced to make his fortune by murder and pillage. The hero is betrayed by a clever woman and acquires a male boon companion who hates women and vies with them for favors. Even when gravely wounded, Umslopogaas' companion Galazi will not abide a woman's touch, especially the touch of one who loves his friend. ("For neither then nor at any other time did Galazi turn to women, but he hated Zinita most of them all" [152].) After one narrow escape Eric and his misogynist companion Skallagrim are discovered unconscious "locked like lovers in each other's arms" (176). In *Nada* Umslopogaas and Galazi live for a long time as savage marauders, hunting with a pack of wolves. Eric and Skallagrim turn pirate. Both books feature ax murderers prone to run amok: "My axe hung on the wainscot. I snatched it thence, and of what befell I know this alone, that when the madness passed, eight men lay stretched out before me, and all the place was but a gore of blood."[19]

The parallels between the two books are not simply the result, as some critics have maintained, of Haggard's mindless repetition of a stock formula. They arise from consistent identification of the European past with the African present. His contemporaries regarded Africans as primitive, mired in a savage stage of development through

which Europeans had passed long ago. Treating the hypothesis as
fact, Haggard uses both European past and African present to provide
examples of repressible but ineradicable human desires.

This identification was especially difficult to attain in *Nada* because
of the racial prejudices of his era. The heroine cannot be permitted to
live entirely as a Zulu maiden. It is rumored that she had a Portuguese
grandfather. "Her eyes were softer and larger than those of our people, her hair longer and less tightly curled, and her skin was
lighter—more of the color of pure copper" (61—62). And it had
been her custom "from childhood not to go about as do other girls,
naked except for their girdles, for she would always find some rag or
skin to lie upon her breast." These unnecessary, ridiculous modifica-
tions of physique and behavior are designed to make it easier for
English readers to identify with her. (Haggard himself, who believed
that he had been a Zulu and loved Zulu women in a previous existence, had no such difficulties.) Once the identification is made, the
reader is transported into a world of the imagination in which all
taboos are abolished. Incest, polygamy, cannibalism, nudism,
necrophilia, patricide, fratricide, and general homicide are everyday
occurrences.

Haggard's Appeal to Late-Victorian Readers

It is a question to what extent Rider Haggard was aware of the
darker aspects of his romances. He once wrote that "sexual passion is
the most powerful lever with which to stir the mind of man, for it lies
at the root of all things human."[20] On the other hand, he would have
winced at much of the analysis presented above. In a public lecture in
1899, Haggard denounced immorality in novels written for
adolescents. He told his audience that he had been shocked to pick up
a magazine "and read in it what was known as a slum story, in which,
in the course of eight or ten pages, was set out a synopsis of almost
every vice that affected humanity. There was murder, there was
treachery of the blackest kind, and there were other vices which he
would not name."[21] These were precisely what any modern reader
would find in his own romances which he cheerfully commended to
children. Neither Haggard nor most of his readers saw the hidden
themes with conscious eyes, and in this lay part of the reason for his
enormous popular success. In Africa or in ancient Iceland, the beasts
which Victorians feared to encounter in themselves could be con-
templated at a safe remove.

This explains why Haggard's romances are so much more challenging and sinister than the serious, realistic novels he wrote for adult audiences. The novels, with their star-crossed lovers, lifelong passions, lifelong sorrows, and exquisitely plotted revenges, suppress the elemental themes unleashed in the romances. To be sure, some of those themes lie just below the surface of the novels. *Dawn, The Witch's Head,* and *Beatrice* feature fierce sibling hostilities; the misogynist boon companion of the romances also appears in *The Witch's Head;* many of the novels pair opposed female characters—one powerful, immoral, and intellectual; the other submissive, pure, and intuitive. But none of the novels begins to approach the romances in bloodshed, horror, or mental pathology.

Haggard and the Psychoanalysts

If all Haggard had done were to provide innocuous outlets for repressed desires, it would be easy to place him in a familiar category. Bram Stoker's vampires whose horror derives from their supposed ability to force their victims into taking delicious delight in unnatural practices, the ghosts concocted by M. R. James and Henry James, and a legion of incubi and succubi belong to this genre. So do the good Indians and "bad Injuns" in whose visages romantics divined the features of the Dionysian and demoniac savages buried deep within European bosoms.[22] What sets Haggard apart, what put him into Freud's dreams rather than onto his couch is the theory of personality which the romances embody—a theory more interesting and elaborate than Stevenson's conception of Jekyll and Hyde. Haggard set the theory out in a rustic way in Quatermain's speech about the twenty parts of the self. "If we would readily understand ourselves" we "must look to the nineteen savage portions of our nature." The theory is adumbrated more elegantly and intricately in the quests for lost civilizations and treasures. Like Freud, who conceptualized the self as a three-tiered structure of superego, ego, and id, Haggard portrays three layers in the human personality. As the landscape changes in Haggard's quests, so do the personalities of his European characters. On the road to King Solomon's mines, Zu-Vendis, Kor, or wherever, the layers progressively fall away. First to go is the top five percent of official civilization. It is as unserviceable as Captain Good's immaculate clothing in the bushlands of the imagination. With the top layer off, the Englishman and African are equal, more fit to fight side by side than against one another. Leopard skins and ostrich feathers are appropriate dress for both. Beneath the layer of official civilization brothers are always rivals, sisters are sworn enemies, sons are rejected by fathers whom they subsequently replace, homosexual love is as common and as passionate as the heterosexual variety. Still deeper, beneath the second layer of personality lurks a third, elemental and horrific, which is literally unconscious. In the heat of battle, Haggard's combatants, whether Zulu, Viking, or English, succumb to bloodlust—go berserk—and kill without restraint until consciousness vanishes behind a sanguinary mist.

Jung conceived of personality in another way which also accords well with Haggard's implicit model. For Jung the personality comprises a layered structure but with a time dimension. Beneath a top layer of present consciousness (including awareness of the demands of official civilization) lies a realm of historic past (including childhood) and a subterranean level of prehistoric or racial past (the collective unconscious). Haggard's adventurers proceed from present-day Europe toward an encounter with the past in Africa. The past they encounter is their own past. Centuries, even millennia, are stripped away in the course of each quest. Significantly, Haggard's Africa teems with the ruins of white civilizations, quite unlike real Africa, which, apart from the Nile Valley and Zimbabwe, is singularly bare of monumental ruins. Under Africa's spell, English gentlemen regress and become Vikings; Cambridge rowers become ancient Greeks.[23]

Haggard and Jung both owed debts to the pioneering British anthropologists Andrew Lang and Sir James Frazer. In the 1880s Lang had anticipated Frazer's argument that apparently irrational elements of contemporary social practice could be explained by investigating their origins in bygone eras. In a series of elegant essays Lang argued that remnants of savage practices and modes of thought survived in modern civilized societies.[24] He also believed that by studying the life of present-day "savages" it was possible to reconstruct part of the lives of our ancestors in the evolutionary process. It was not simply because he wished to encourage escapism in literature that he greeted Haggard's work with such enthusiasm. He perceived that Haggard was working out in fiction the implications of his own work in comparative mythology. Jung expanded this idea to include the doctrine that the psyche as well as society retained remnants of the ancestral past.

Both Freud and Jung follow Haggard in using metaphors of landscape to describe the discovery of new facets of the self. Haggard takes his reader through swamps, dense woods, or desert to a mountainous landscape where caves or caverns must first be negotiated before the journey's goal is spectacularly revealed in a bird's-eye view.[25] Freud does the same thing in the theatrical opening to the vital third chapter of his *Interpretation of Dreams*: "When, after passing through a narrow defile, we suddenly emerge upon a piece of high ground, where the path divides and the finest prospects open up on every side, we may pause for a moment and consider in which direction we shall first turn our steps." In a letter to his friend Wilhelm Fliess, Freud sharpened and extended the metaphor: "The whole thing [his book] is planned on the model of an imaginary walk. First comes the dark wood of the authorities . . . where there is no clear view and it is easy to go astray. Then there is a cavernous defile through which I lead my readers . . . and then, all at once, the high ground and the open prospect and the question: 'Which way do you want to go?' "[26] Dreams were for Freud the "royal road to the unconscious." The perilous path to his own "immortal works" led through Haggard's landscape.

Jung in his turn spoke of Freud's "passion for knowledge which was to lay open a dark continent to his gaze."[27] Jung, with his concept of a "collective unconscious," was much closer than Freud to Haggard's identification of the savage pasts of civilized men with the "savages" of the other dark continent. L. F. A. Maury had speculated in 1878 that man reverts to "the state of nature" when he dreams: Havelock Ellis thought that the study of dreams might reveal "primitive stages in the evolution of mental life."[28] Jung carried this line of speculation to extremes. Inspired writers might catch "a glimpse of the psychic world that terrifies the primitive and is at the same time his greatest hope."[29] The archetypes about which Jung wrote so confidently (and vaguely) he illustrated, like Lang, sometimes with references to our unknown ancestors, sometimes with references to living "primitive men."[30] It did not occur to Jung that his admiration for Haggard arose from their common adherence to the theory of the layered personality. Jung treated Haggard's romances as raw psychological material which verified the truth of his own superior insight:

In general, it is the non-psychological novel that offers the richest opportunities for psychological elucidation . . . Good examples of such novels are those of Benoit, or English fiction after the manner of Rider Haggard. . . . An exciting narrative that is apparently quite devoid of psychological intentions is just what interests the psychologist most of all. Such a tale is constructed against a background of unspoken psychological assumptions, and the more unconscious the author is of them, the more the background reveals itself in unalloyed purity to the discerning eye.[31]

So *She* appears in a select list of works of art which reveal a world of "primordial experiences" and "primal beginnings" transcending the conscious intentions of their creators, a list which includes Dante's *Divine Comedy*, Goethe's *Faust*, and Richard Wagner's *Ring*.

Without in any way denigrating the power of Haggard's imagination, it is possible to take another view of his achievement. Haggard's romances were immensely popular because they fed the imagination of a vast reading public that had already accepted the premises, but not the conclusions, of the looming Viennese psychology. As Ernest Jones has observed, the idea of an unconscious mind was casually expounded in many places in the last two decades of the nineteenth century; the shock of Freud lay in the content rather than the concept of the unconscious.[32] Rider Haggard would have been prepared for that shock despite his honest protestations of rectitude. He knew that the key to self-knowledge lay in "the nineteen savage parts" and that "sexual passion lies at the root of all things human." Though he did not know to what extent he had written those notions into his novels, a Freud or Jung could see them at once. What they saw was not, however, a confirmation of their daring theories but a reflection of them.[33] Again and again Haggard marches virtuous men into the wilderness where they reveal hidden savage impulses and confront the awesome mysteries of their deepest inner selves.

Imperialism and the Early Romances

The subject of Haggard's politics will be treated at length in a later chapter, but it is appropriate at this point to say just a word about imperialism. While there is no political or economic imperialism in Haggard's early romances, the instinct which would place them among "novels of empire" is not entirely mistaken. The imperial situation made a grand metaphorical stage for encounters and battles between different sections of the self. Conrad used it to play out the tragedy of civilized egos tempted and destroyed by savages within. His Kurtz went to the Congo to bear the white man's burden and finished by succumbing to the darkness in his own psyche, which responded all too readily to its external manifestation in the black African. Imperialism for Conrad is the price one pays for civilization—the repression of savagery at home and abroad.

This notion is closely related to Freud's view that without repression civilization would dissolve. Rider Haggard wrote less self-consciously and consequently placed less emphasis on the role of the imperial ego. Command and rule are underplayed. Succumbing to and identifying with the savage are vital ingredients in the reiterated formula of his exotic tales. It may be that Haggard's own need for self-revelation led him to take this approach. As we have seen in chapter 1, the adolescent Haggard was so self-contained that his parents thought him dull.[34] His early unsuccessful novels contain a few thinly disguised episodes from his painful early manhood, but his autobiography is distinctly unrevealing. The European characters of Haggard's romances do what he could not do. They dive deeply into African darkness and emerge shaken but refreshed. This different use of the imperial situation in his novels helps to explain the paradox that Haggard skirted imperialism in his romances and preached it on the platform while Conrad excoriated imperialism in politics and bowed down before the imperial idea in his books.

Chapter Four
The Later Romances

Haggard wrote thirty-six more "romances" and a score of short stories. None of them equaled the popular success of *She, King Solomon's Mines,* or *Allan Quatermain.* Many of them depict further adventures of Ayesha, Allan, and Umslopopgaas. Confronted with these bare facts, many critics have not bothered to read through the daunting pile of books. They have jumped to the conclusion that Haggard's later works were ground out like so many identical sausages. Malcolm Elwin considered that *People of the Mist* (1894) was "the first of many pot-boilers produced to feed the public created by his early successes." A mid-twentieth-century reviewer suggested that it was "Haggard's sedulous determination to repeat his early success that makes his later books so tiresome." Another branded him a bore who "mechanically manufactured imitations." The "fact that a number of these ill-written books are still in print" he considered nothing more than "an interesting sociological fact."[1]

There are at least three good reasons to question these offhand judgments. One is that even Haggard's detractors grant that his writing improved with practice. Another is that if the later romances were in fact carbon copies of the earlier ones, it would be difficult to explain why successive generations of readers have preferred the former to the latter. A third is that close study will reveal that Haggard did not repeat the plot lines of his first three great successes. The later romances are indeed repetitious but they repeat other formulas. This chapter will first consider the charge of bad writing so often leveled against Haggard and will then examine examples of each of the broad categories into which the later romances fall. An attempt will be made to explain why those works were less appealing to the book-buying public and to relate this declining appeal to the contrasting fortunes of the novels and romances described in the previous two chapters. The principal argument will be that there was a gradual convergence between the themes of the later romances and the obsessive concerns of Haggard's realistic novels.

Good and Bad Writing

The first full-length academic study of Haggard's life was Morton Cohen's *Rider Haggard* (1960). It attempted to explain why his books had attracted so many outstanding literary people despite what Cohen regarded as serious flaws in Haggard's style. Cohen charged that he was "in the main a hasty writer" and often "a bored and tired writer" whose "sentence structure is frequently cumbersome and unnecessarily involved"; a writer, furthermore, who did "not command the variety of words and images" needed "to make his prose engaging."[2] A more recent study by P. B. Ellis (1978) was undertaken specifically for the purpose of refuting Cohen's appraisal. Ellis found it "impossible to seriously accept that any weaknesses that occur in Haggard's literary style 'stand between him and immortality.' . . . What other word but 'immortal' can describe *She* and *King Solomon's Mines* which inspired over a dozen film versions, stage productions, radio serials, an opera and even a ballet? Several times they have been transcribed to comic-strip forms and printed as full colour comic books, the most recent of which has appeared, even as I write, from Marvel Comics."[3]

It is easy to see that Ellis is unwittingly arguing at cross purposes with Cohen in this exchange. "Immortality" achieved through radio serials and comic books has nothing to do with literary excellence. And Cohen fully acknowledges the power of Haggard's imagination. On the other hand, he goes too far in denigrating Haggard's prose style. In the vast corpus of the novels and romances, there are plentiful examples to be found of both good and bad prose. On the credit side of the ledger there are passages which demonstrate great economy of expression and a keen awareness of multiple levels of meaning. Consider, for example Haggard's description in *The Ghost Kings* of young Rachel's awakening consciousness of her womanhood. The girl, who will later be mistaken by the Zulus for their legendary goddess of the heavens who rides on the lightning, is about to be caught in a thunderstorm:

The atmosphere was full of electricity struggling to be free. Although she knew not what it was, Rachel felt it in her blood and brain. In some strange way it affected her mind, opening windows there through which the eyes of her soul looked out. (11)

The electricity is both in Rachel and in the sky. It foreshadows the main theme of the book at the same time that it sets the immediate stage for Rachel's first encounter with her predestined lover.

Among dozens of examples that might be given of Haggard's excellence in the depiction of landscape is his word-picture of the chasm through which the adventurers of *Allan Quatermain* pass on their way to Zu-Vendis:

Our river . . . was running on its darksome way, not now through "caverns measureless to man," but between two frightful cliffs which cannot have been less than two thousand feet high. So high were they, indeed, that though the sky was above us, where we were was dense gloom—not darkness, indeed, but the gloom of a room closely shuttered in the daytime. Up on either side rose the great straight cliffs, grim and forbidding, till the eye grew dizzy with trying to measure their sheer height. The little space of sky that marked where they ended lay like a thread of blue upon their soaring blackness which was unrelieved by any tree or creeper. Here and there, however, grew ghostly patches of a long grey lichen, hanging motionless to the rock as the white beard to the chin of a dead man. It seemed as though only the dregs or heavier part of the light had sunk to the bottom of this awful place. No bright-winged sunbeam could fall so low: they died far, far above our heads. (112-13)

Another sort of writing in which Haggard shone was the production of literally spine-chilling climaxes. The lines in *Swallow* which describe Ralph's discovery of a mountain he had seen in a dream are as nicely calculated as Arthur Conan Doyle's famous lead up to the line, "They were the footprints of a gigantic hound!"

On the other hand there is no gainsaying those who point to convincing counterexamples of awkward and hasty writing. As often as he excels in scene painting, Haggard will say that "it is impossible to describe" some beautiful or awe-inspiring sight. "Hewn from the living rock" is his almost invariable phrase for depicting ancient cave sculptures. His plotting can be clumsily contrived, as in this passage from *The Ancient Allan* in which two characters discuss someone well known to both of them:

"Do you remember the old hermit, the holy Tanoufir, who dwells in a cell over the sepulchre of the Apis bulls in the burial ground of the desert near to Memphis, Bes?"

"The magician and prophet who is the brother of your grandfather, Master, and the son of a king; he who brought you up before he became a hermit? Yes, I know him. . . ." (93)

But when all is said that can be said, this debate on the good and bad in Haggard's prose will not help to fix its place in the history of literature. The most severe of Haggard's critics grants that "his later work does become more fluent and taut, as narrative kinks and some of the stylistic faults disappear."[4] Men of good literary judgment—Kipling, Lang, and Walter Besant—noticed the same steady improvement. Yet it is not the later "better" works that today's readers will see among new books for sale. They will see the first "ill-written" romances. So it is not to any deterioration of skill but to the changed content of Haggard's later romances that one must look for the explanation of their declining popular appeal.

Lost City Romances

The theme of lost worlds and lost civilizations which won such widespread acclaim in *King Solomon's Mines, Allan Quatermain,* and *She* was repeated again and again in later works. However, the characters and plot lines of these tales undergo significant changes. A party of co-equal adventurers figures in each of the first three great romances. Little is said about the past of these characters, their parentage, upbringing, or previous romantic entanglements. The narrator takes no part in the love affairs which occur. There are no sibling romances or rivalries among the adventurers. There are no immortal triangles. The original object of the expedition tends to be forgotten in the course of the action and the characters seriously consider settling down in the strange world they find.

People of the Mist (1894) tells of a quite different quest. Leonard Outram and his brother are dispossessed of their ancestral home because of the debts piled up by their dead father. The extensive estates are sold to a Jew. The father of Leonard's intended bride Jane Beach forbids his daughter to have anything more to do with the now penniless gentleman and encourages her to marry the Jew. At their tearful final meeting, Jane promises to remain true to Leonard. He and his brother bind themselves by a solemn oath to devote their lives to reclaiming their patrimony. They go off prospecting for gold in southern Africa. After years of backbreaking work, Leonard alone survives and has precious little gold to show for it. At the point of giving up, he is approached by a mysterious African woman, Soa. She asks his help in rescuing her white mistress from slave traders who have sacked the settlement where she had lived with her outcast father, a drunken trader. Soa promises to reward his efforts by leading him to the rubies mined by her people who live in a secluded mountain kingdom far away. Aided by his dedicated servant Otter, a clever but very ugly Zulu dwarf, Leonard makes his way into the slavers' camp disguised as a French buyer. They arrive just in time to witness the auction of Juanna the captured white girl. With his hard-won gold Leonard makes the highest bid and is then forced by the sadistic slaving chief to be married on the spot by a disreputable Portuguese priest. In a bloody aftermath Leonard and Otter raise a slave revolt and make a daring escape with Juanna, Soa, and the priest as the island encampment is engulfed by flames.

This ill-assorted party then proceeds to Soa's kingdom. En route Juanna pretends indifference to Leonard's wooing, partly because she resents the marriage she was forced to undergo at the slave camp, and partly because she believes that Leonard secretly pines for Jane in England. To complicate matters, Soa the servant and Francisco the priest become jealous of Leonard because they too are smitten with love for Juanna. Their stratagem for winning the rubies, which requires Juanna and the dwarf Otter to impersonate gods, falls apart when the intensity of Soa's lesbian jealousy causes her to reveal the masquerade to the high priest of the local cult. To save Juanna, Francisco puts on her clothes and is precipitated along with Otter into the pool of the sacred crocodile. Otter kills the beast and leads his friends to safety across a perilous bridge of ice. Though they do not carry away any rubies, they end up rich and reasonably happy in England thanks to the munificence of Jane Beach. During Leonard's absence she had bowed to her father's wishes and married the Jew. He died soon afterward and left the ancient Outram estates to her. She in turn followed him to the grave, leaving everything to Leonard. In an epilogue more bizarre than any of his previous African adventures, Leonard is seen ten years later, a knighted member of Parliament and lord lieutenant of his county. Otter, "dressed in a white smock, stands behind his master's chair" at a formal dinner. Juanna is the mother of four adorable children. Her secret sadness is that she must live in "the shadow of a woman, a woman sweet and pale, who, as she believed stood between her and that which she desired above all things—the complete and absolute possession of her husband's heart" (341-43).

Is this a mindless potboiler hastily written to feed the popular appetite for more lost mines? On first inspection it may appear to be so. Rubies are substituted for diamonds as the object of the quest. There is a physical test of courage to be undergone at the slave camp before the expedition to an undiscovered country can get under way. Two of the party impersonate gods, as did the heroes of *King Solomon's Mines*. Haggard concocts an anthropology for the "people of the mist" out of bits and pieces of past and present societies, much as he had done in earlier romances. They are "between black and yellow in hue," monogamous in marriage, and fond of watching human sacrifices in a vast amphitheater which calls to mind "a Roman audience gathered to witness a gladiatorial show." More important than these superficial resemblances, however, are the substantial differences between *People of the Mist* and its predecessors. The composition of this party of adventurers is far different from that which went to Kukuanaland and Zu-Vendis. Leonard and Otter are more like Robinson Crusoe and his man Friday than they are like Allan Quatermain and Ignosi. The servant goes because his master goes, not because he has a quest of his own. This, the gold mine, and the slave encampment bring the realities of European colonialism more to the fore than had been the case in earlier romances. Otter's unfitness to function in any other than a subordinate position is demonstrated in the mountain kingdom where he bungles his impersonation of a god by drinking and wenching. Furthermore, Leonard's search for the rubies is simply an extension of his frankly mercenary gold-digging. The addition of Soa and Juanna to the party drags a heavy extra freight of romantic complications into the story which eventually outweighs the quest as the central theme of the book. Changes of identity are superficial rather than profound. Although Leonard is said at one point to have "grown primitive"—"his mind was as the mind of a Norseman or of an Aztec"—he never really steps out of character (34). Even when he must act the part of brutalized slaver, he forgets "to preserve the truculent expression which it was his part to wear. Once more Leonard's face was the face of an English gentleman, noble and open, if somewhat stern" (87). So it continues to be throughout the rest of the tale.

There *are* repetitions of earlier Haggard stories in *People of the Mist*, but they do not come from the first wildly successful romances. They come from the unsuccessful novels. Leonard Outram is a figure met before in *Dawn* and *Witch's Head*. Cut off from his patrimony, he is jilted while in Africa and even after his rehabilitation he persists in believing that his destiny is mysteriously, eternally entangled with his first lost love. He is another version of Ernest Kershaw and Arthur Heigham. That is to say, he is another version of Rider Haggard. By inserting his old obsession into *People of the Mist*, Haggard drastically altered the message of the quest.

There are similar shifts in content in the later romances concerning
"She-Who-Must-Be-Obeyed." In *Ayesha, The Return of She* (1905)
Leo Vincey and Horace Holly pursue Ayesha's reincarnation in Central Asia. Sixteen years of wandering have changed them in mind and
body. Leo no longer resembles an empty-headed Greek body builder:
"His hair had grown long . . . a curling golden mane, as his great
beard hung upon his breast, spreading outwards almost to the
massive shoulders. The face too . . . was beautiful though burnt
brown with weather; refined and full of thought, sombre almost, and
in it clear as crystal, steady as stars, shone his large grey eyes" (34). He
and Holly study Buddhism before finding their way to a forgotten
kingdom ruled by descendants of soldiers who accompanied Alex-
ander the Great on his Eastern campaign. The kingdom is oddly split
into physically separate realms of church and state. The state is controlled by the beautiful Atene, Khania of Kaloon, who acts on behalf
of her mad, bad husband. Religion is controlled from a nearby
volcano by the priestess Hesea who is said to be immortal. Hesea is of
course She. The Khania recognizes Leo as one for whom she has been
waiting and tries to keep him as her own lover. Leo, though slightly
tempted, insists on going on to the sacred volcano.

There he finds that She too has changed. Though living, she is old
and shriveled. When Leo demonstrates his continued devotion
despite her decrepit appearance, she reciprocates by calling up the
sacred fire and clothing herself in ethereal beauty. Maddeningly, she
holds Leo at arm's length, insisting that the time for the uniting of
bodies and spirits has not yet arrived. Khania Atene further delays
this consummation by using a subterfuge to capture Leo and carry
him to her capital. Ayesha exacts a swift and terrible revenge with an
invading army of tempests and ghosts which lays the kindgom waste.
After this second hard-won reunion, Leo will not stand for any further
delays and demands a kiss. The physical contact is instantly fatal.
Ayesha carries his corpse into the heart of the volcano, promising
before she goes to collect Holly later in England.

Although the subtitle *The Return of She* promises readers a spine-
tingling rerun of the original story, the book is far from being a
"mechanical imitation." The character of Ayesha has been altered
almost beyond recognition. When Holly saw her at Kor, her beauty
with all its awful loveliness and purity, was *evil*." She was a
thoroughgoing Darwinian who dismissed all orthodox religions as
weak-kneed follies. Now she wears a visible halo "of gentle radiance
on her brow." She preaches that beneath their superficial

dissimilarities "all great Faiths are the same," all are manifestation of the "one Power great and good" who "rules all the universes." "The holy shall inherit a life eternal and the vile, eternal death" (279). The central symbol of her old domain had been a statue of Truth, veiled because it cannot be known. In her second home the central symbol is a representation of "universal Motherhood." Only occasionally does Ayesha step out of her newfound role as a nondenominational Sunday school teacher and show flashes of the old ruthless brilliance: once when she proposes to use her mastery of alchemy to make Leo monarch of a worldwide empire with its capital at Peking, and again when she devastates all Kaloon in order to crush a single enemy.

Haggard accomplishes this transformation of Ayesha by transferring most of her former evil qualities to her rival Atene. Like Ustane in *She*, Atene is portrayed as a reincarnation of the ancient Amenartas, wife of Kallikrates. Ustane, however, was a simple, gentle creature whose only offence against Ayesha was her selfless love for Leo. Atene, on the other hand, is a hardened sinner, wise in the ways of adultery and lust. Compared to Ayesha, Leo tells Holly, Atene's "voice sounded coarse; yes she grew almost vulgar" while "when Ayesha was in a rage she might be wicked as we understand it, and was certainly terrible, but she was never either coarse or vulgar, any more than lightning is" (122). Haggard offers nothing more than a lame suggestion of an explanation for the startling change in his famous character. It is implied that long ago she made a bargain with the devil, whose sinful consequences she is expiating in the course of successive reincarnations. The introduction of Eastern religion with its notions of karma and striving after godliness in progressive existences strengthens this suggestion. But it fatally weakens the novel. The original She had been a magnificent character who fascinated late Victorians with her stunning combination of heavenly beauty and diabolical amorality. Shorn of her atheism, her sexuality, and her merciless exercise of power, she shrinks to the stature of an ordinary Haggard heroine. The story becomes just another tale of a man who is torn between two women and who must seek ultimate fulfillment beyond the grave—another tale of the old obsession.

A later lost-city romance, *She and Allan* (1921) shows Ayesha in the same guise even though it is set in a time prior to the first adventure of *She*. The book was plainly an attempt by Haggard to woo his public back to him with a ripping yarn of their three favorite characters, Allan Quatermain, Ayesha, and Umslopogaas. None of them, however, behave much like their original selves. Allan is feeling blue because he misses the women whom death has taken away from him. He consults a Zulu diviner, hoping to learn whether he will meet them hereafter. The witch doctor refers him to a white queen in the far north who can tell the future. Umslopogaas comes along because he has temporarily lost his characteristic stoicism about death and wants to know whether *he* will ever be reunited with his lost love Nada. On the way they become entangled in a subplot which Haggard had used many times before. They run into a drunken European trader who has "gone native" and whose beautiful daughter has been kidnapped by a vicious raiding party. In this case the raiders represent an evil giant named Rezu who rules half the kingdom of Kor. He intends to set the stolen girl up as a rival queen to Ayesha. Allan and Umslopogaas rescue the girl, kill the giant, and are rewarded by Ayesha with a potion that sends them briefly off to the world of the dead where they partially satisfy their mystic yearnings.

Ayesha plays only a small part in the book, but when she speaks it is with the voice of a religious seer rather than a Nietzschean evolutionist. The deletion of her less admirable characteristics forced Haggard to introduce the giant Rezu into the story to maintain a dramatic contest between forces of good and evil. Readers of *She* were encouraged to shudder at prospect of Ayesha's remorseless despotic rule being extended to the British isles. In *She and Allan* Ayesha is recast as the good ruler. Even more remarkable are the changes wrought in Allan and Umslopogaas. Schoolboy readers of *King Solomon's Mines* and *Allan Quatermain* must have been amazed to find their thick-skinned heroes mooning about in search of a drug which will put them in touch with dead lovers.

At the opening of the book, Allan attempts an explanation of his altered state by once again invoking the theory of multiple personalities.

I believe it was the old Egyptians . . . who declared that each individual personality is made up of six or seven different elements. . . . The body that the man or woman wore . . . was but a kind of sack or fleshly covering containing these different principles. Or mayhap it did not contain them at all, but was simply a house as it were, in which they lived from time to time and seldom all together, although one or more of them was present continually, as though to keep the place warm and aired. . . .

Anyhow of one thing I am quite sure, we are not always the same. Different personalities actuate us at different times. In one hour passion of this sort or the other is our lord; in another we are reason itself. In one hour we follow the basest appetites; in another we hate them and the spirit arising through our mortal murk shines within or above us like a star. In one hour our desire is to kill and spare not; in another we are filled with the holiest compassion even towards an insect or a snake and are ready to forgive like a god. Everything rules us in turn, to such an extent indeed, that sometimes one begins to wonder whether we really rule anything (13-14).

However, the theory of multiple personalities is not employed and dramatized in *She and Allan* as it had been in the early romances. Quatermain does not reveal new facets of his personality as he advances toward Kor. He does not become a savage. He maintains his temporary character of world-weariness. When he lies down at last, eager to precipitate himself into the Hereafter, he is simply another version of Morris Monk, the anemic hero of Haggard's "realistic" novel *Stella Fregelius*.

   Heart of the World (1896) was another romance of lost cities which descends from *People of the Mist* rather than from the more celebrated earlier adventures. The core of the plot concerns the developing love affair between an English mining engineer and a Mexican Indian princess as they trek towards her mountain home. At the golden city their love is thwarted by the jealousies of rivals, male and female, and by the machinations of a cruel priesthood. There is nothing very strange or interesting about the anthropology of the lost world. What Haggard emphasizes in his description of its people is the lassitude induced by their failure to expand and to incorporate new elements in the kingdom:

The blood of the people grew old, and but few children were born to them. There were none left upon the mainland to replenish the race. . . . before another hundred years have been added to the past, the city, Heart of the World, must become nothing but a waste and a home for the dead . . . for the people have no thought for the morrow, and the hearts of its nobles have become gross and their eyes blind. (136—37)

   This shift in emphasis is as important as the change in characterization noted above. Haggard is no longer using his lost peoples as titillating examples of what we might become without the restraints of conventional morality. He is using them to preach a cautionary tale of what might become of the English should they lose contact with their empire and devote themselves to selfish vanities and pleasures— they will decline and fall. It was a theme that spoke to the anxieties of

many of his contemporaries, and to which he would return many
times in later novels. But it was a theme which other authors address-
ed at greater length and with greater success. Like the shift in person-
nel in his quests, the change of theme did not represent a mechanical
repetition of stories which had sold well. It represented another instance of Haggard indulging his personal hobbyhorses in books which
a considerable number of readers would buy simply because his name
was on the cover.

Historical Romances

Haggard once complained that the progress of exploration was
rapidly depleting his supply of exotic settings. "Soon," he lamented
in 1894, "the ancient mystery of Africa will have vanished." Where
then "will the romance writers of future generations find a safe and
secret place, unknown to the pestilent accuracy of the geographer, in
which to lay their plots?"[5] Aside from Central Asia there were only
the planets and other galaxies in prospect. He neglected to mention
the past, another "safe and secret place" which he had barely touched in his novels up to 1894 but to which he often turned in later life.
Eric Brighteyes had been an exercise in saga writing without any firm
anchor in chronology. *The World's Desire* which mated Odysseus and
Helen of Troy was pure fantasy. *Nada* and *Cleopatra* had skirted
round the known facts of Zulu and Egyptian history. *Montezuma's
Daughter* (1893) was Haggard's first wholehearted effort at writing
historical romance.

The milieu, Mexico in the era of the Spanish conquest, was a
natural for the author of *Allan Quatermain*. A handful of adventurers
accompanied Cortez to a mountain kingdom where they were hailed
as god conquerors by the priests and rulers of a city on a lake. (No
doubt Haggard had had the Aztec kingdom in mind when he constructed the imaginary realm of Zu-Vendis.)[6] After his treasure-
seeking trip to Mexico he attempted the real thing. The telling of the
story presented obvious difficulties. It would be unthinkable for Haggard, whose previous romances emphasized identification with
"savage peoples," to side with the Spanish. On the other hand, he
had never attempted to view resistance to European conquest directly
through the eyes of the conquered. His solution to the problem was to
invent a half-Spanish Englishman, Thomas Wingfield, who travels to
Mexico in pursuit of a Spanish enemy of his family. He is captured by
the Aztecs and forced to impersonate a god for a year, at the end of

which time he is to be sacrificed along with the four "wives" who have ministered to his pleasures during his sham godhood. This gives him a grandstand seat at the conquest. The final Spanish assault occurs on the day ordained for his sacrifice which enables him to manage a hair's breadth escape along with one of his "wives," Montezuma's own daughter, with whom he has fallen truly in love. They make their way to her mother's people and rule their own isolated mountain kingdom until the long arm of Spanish imperialism reaches out to crush them.

The book was written at a low point in Haggard's life. His son had just died and his marriage was on the verge of ending altogether in the physical sense. Grief and guilt consumed him. He was even more than usually frank about writing himself into the plot. Thomas Wingfield is cast as a younger son of the owner of Ditchingham House, Norfolk, the property Haggard acquired through his marriage to Louise Margitson. Wingfield is mistreated by his father and his elder brother. His vendetta against the family enemy is undertaken to vindicate his mother whom he idolizes. To pursue the villain he must leave his true love Lily, whose father is pushing her into marriage with a richer man. Across the seas Wingfield has affairs and even marries the noble daughter of the Aztec emperor but he never entirely forgets Lily. He returns to her after the death of his Indian wife and his beloved eldest son. But of course now he is constantly thinking of the other love "which death has completed sealing it for ever and making it immortal" (16). By the end of the story the character who was invented merely to make the plot work has largely overshadowed the grand, sad spectacle of the Aztec downfall. Once again the private griefs of the author had been allowed to impede the free working of his imagination.

Swallow (1899) is an historical romance in an altogether different vein. Set in South Africa during the eighteen thirties, it takes up a theme first announced ten years earlier in *Allan's Wife:* love in the African wilds temporarily thwarted by a villainous kidnapper. In this case it is the love between an Afrikaner girl, Suzanne Botmar, and a young English castaway, Ralph Mackenzie, which is interrupted by Swart Piet Van Vooren, a Boer of partly African descent (who calls to mind Frank Muller in *Jess.*) Through the help of her devoted companion, the black seer Sihamba, Suzanne escapes the repellent embraces of Swart Piet. The two women fly for refuge to Sihamba's ancestral home on the "Mountain of the Man's Hand" where she resumes her rightful place as queen of a small tribe of cowards. Even-

tually when the evil machinations of Swart Piet causes a Zulu raiding
party to attack their mountain, Sihamba arranges for Suzanne to
escape by smearing her with black grease and smuggling her out
disguised as a young African mother. A series of coincidences reunites
her with Ralph and together they return to the mountain to rescue
Sihamba but arrive just after she has been murdered by Swart Piet.

At the time the book appeared it was praised by one reviewer as
"immensely superior" to anything Haggard had previously written.
Later critics have been less impressed with its literary excellence,
noting it merely as evidence of an interesting evolution in Haggard's
political opinions, inasmuch as it paints a far more attractive picture
of the Afrikaner (Boer) people than *Cetywayo* or *Jess*.[7] There are good
reasons for recognizing merit in the earlier judgment and for modify-
ing the later one. *Swallow* does stand a cut above most of Haggard's
later novels. It continually surprises the reader with unexpected turn-
ings and departs from the usual preoccupations of the author. Srecham-
ba is pretty and clever and lacking in the vicious lesbian jealousy that
Haggard generally ascribed to the black companions of the heroines of
his African adventures (for example in *Allan's Wife, People of the
Mist,* and *Finished*). As history it stands alone among white fiction of
southern Africa.

Despite its subtitle, *A Tale of the Great Trek,* and Haggard's effective use of an old Boer woman as the narrator, the book hardly
touches on the famous Afrikaner invasion of the High Veld country.
The backdrop is really the time of "the crushing" which followed the
rise of the Zulu monarchy, the time which the Nguni call the *Mfecane*
and the Sotho call the *Difaqane*. For small tribes caught in this
maelstrom of war and forced migration, life was solitary, poor, nasty,
brutish, and short. Haggard captures the spirit of the time very well.
His brave black queen is loosely modeled on MaNthatisi of the
Tlokwa. Her mountain refuge resembles the fortress home of
Moshweshwe who built the Basuto nation during this period by
gathering the flotsam and jetsam of uprooted African humanity who
had been cast adrift by the *Difaqane*. Only the black author Sol Plaatje has written so informed and sympathetic a fictional account of that
era.[8] This, rather than the fragmentary references to the Great Boer
Trek, makes *Swallow* one of the best historical romances to come out
of South Africa.

The racial undertones of the book are complex. On the one hand,
the evil of Swart Piet is attributed directly to his half-African parentage. "With round Kaffir eyes, black and cruel, coarse black hair that

grew low on his brow, full red lips, the lower drooping so that the large white teeth and a line of gums could be seen within," the man shows "in his face the cruelty and the cunning of a black race, mingled with the mind and mastery of the white" (94). On the other hand, Sihamba is portrayed as equal or superior to Suzanne in every respect. When the white girl is painted black, she feels humiliated, but Africans admire the effect. "Wow," one exclaims, "she who was white as snow has become black as coal, and yes, she looks best black" (290). These complicated and ambivalent attitudes show up as well in Haggard's three novels which recount the decline and fall of the house of Shaka. It is on these books, rather than the novels of early modern Europe and Mexico, that Haggard's reputation as a writer of historical fiction ultimately rests.

The Zulu Trilogy

Haggard's faithful publisher and friend Charles Longman gave his own opinion about the reasons for the diminishing popularity of the romances in 1907. "I hanker after another King Solomon or Allan Quatermain. Hunting, adventure, some of the peculiar vein of humour of those early yarns, romance—all these I can do with, but no mystics, if you please. Now you know just the sort of book I want and there are lots of other thick heads who want just the same." Haggard's answer to this summons came in 1909 when he wrote in rapid succession *Child of Storm* and *Marie*. Before their publication in 1912 and 1913, Haggard was able to consult with James Stuart who had served as Secretary for Native Affairs in Natal and had collected a mass of oral tradition concerning early Zulu history. This refreshed and enriched his own memories which were now thirty years old. The final volume in the trilogy, *Finished*, appeared in 1917 after Haggard had revisited Natal as part of the Dominions Royal Commission.[9] From these old and new materials he constructed the trilogy around three pivotal events in the later history of the Zulu kings: the contest between the Voortrekkers and Dingane in 1838; the civil war between Mpande's sons Mbulazi and Cetshwayo in 1856; and the Anglo-Zulu War of 1879.

In order to satisfy Longman and others who demanded the resurrection of Allan Quatermain, Haggard used the white hunter as a unifying element, rather than the black narrator who had served him so well in *Nada the Lily*. This in turn demanded an adjustment in the age of Allan (said in *King Solomon's Mines* to have been fifty-five in

1885). In *Marie* he appears as a teenager in the frontier war of 1835. Echoing the plots of *Nada*, *Eric Brighteyes*, and *Swallow*, Allan is in love with a neighbor, Marie Marais, who has been almost a sister to him. In this case she is the daughter of a fanatically anti-British Boer who wishes to marry her off to a swarthy half-Portuguese villain, Hernan Pereira. During the Great Trek, Marie's family accompanies the ill-fated Trigardt party into the disease-ridden interior of western Mozambique. Allan organizes a daring rescue and leads the survivors to a reunion with the main body of the trekkers in Natal. Pereira and Marie's insane father plot with the Zulus in the hope of getting Allan murdered in a general massacre of the Boer embassy to Dingane. Thanks to his English parentage, Allan is spared by the Zulus and is forced to be a helpless witness to the slaughter of Piet Retief and his companions. Later he is accused by Pereira of having been responsible for that disaster. A kangaroo court of ignorant trekkers sentences him to death. Marie saves him by tricking him into taking a sleeping potion, dressing herself in his clothes, and sacrificing herself in his place.

Child of Storm involves Allan in the rivalry between Mpande's sons Cetshwayo and Mbulazi for the right of succession to the Zulu throne. The ambitious scheming of a beautiful lowborn girl—Mameena, "The Zulu Helen"—and the vengeful cunning of an old witch doctor, Zikali, who bears a grudge against the whole royal family, turn the struggle into a full-blown civil war. Allan himself narrowly avoids falling in love with Mameena and watches regretfully as she seduces Prince Mbulazi. After the destruction of his regiments, Cetshwayo condemns her to death. Minutes before she is due to be executed, she claims one last kiss from Allan, during which she swallows poison.

Finished borrows a plot from *People of the Mist* to carry Quatermain into Zululand on the eve of the English invasion. While on a hunting trip with Maurice Anscombe, an English nobleman, he stumbles upon a gang of diamond thieves led by two disgraced gentlemen. The half-Hungarian daughter of one of the crooks falls in love with Anscombe, which arouses the jealousy of her father's partner. She, her lover, and Allan manage a bloody escape. Quatermain has been told in a dream that they can find safety by flying to the witch doctor Zikali in Zululand. Zikali and the man-hating Zulu girl who serves as his assistant force the white woman to impersonate the legendary Queen of the Heavens. At a meeting called by king Cetshwayo to decide whether the nation should go to war with England, Zikali uses the fake goddess to swing the decision in favor of war. In the ensuing confusion Allan is caught up in the battle of Isandhlwana and is one of the few British survivors. Zikali's assistant, who has fallen in love with the white girl, attempts to have Anscombe and Quatermain killed by betraying their hiding place to Cetshwayo but repents at the last minute and sacrifices herself in their place. An epilogue finds Quatermain back in Zululand four years later. Cetshwayo, having witnessed the destruction of his people, dies a lonely death tormented by ghosts and the taunts of Zikali who has lived to see the final ruin of the royal house.

These novels have been extravagantly praised for their historical accuracy. They are said to be "a perfect mirror of the Zulu as he was before he was touched by civilization." One of Haggard's biographers has predicted that "as the African nations continue to take their place in the modern world of states, during the late twentieth century and in the twenty-first, their writers will, if they follow the pattern of those in other new or reborn nations, try to portray the glories of their people's past. Among their sources will most likely be found Haggard's works."[10] Though there is much to commend in his approach to Zulu humanity, these judgments will not stand up to close examination. Haggard disregarded and altered many known facts about Zulu history in order to make his plots work. His unabated idolization of Shepstone caused him to accept without question the Shepstonian interpretation of key events in the life of the Zulu monarchy.

The most serious charge that can be brought in evidence against him is that he trivializes Zulu history by making personalities responsible for changing its course at important junctures. It is not a profound reason of state but Hernan Pereira's desire to destroy Allan Quatermain that Haggard identifies as the efficient cause of Dingane's massacre of the Trekker embassy. It is the ambition of Mameena and the jealousy of one of her discarded rivals rather than lack of a settled principle of succession in the Zulu kingdom that Haggard singles out as the cause of the civil war of 1856. More seriously, the Zulu War is attributed partly to Cetshwayo's alleged disregard of the "promises" made at his coronation by Shepstone in 1873, promises which Haggard knew very well had no status in anyone's law.[11] The Zulu decision to reject Sir Bartle Frere's cynical and impossible ultimatum of December 1879 is attributed to a consultation between Cetshwayo and diviners. This not only gives an entirely false picture of Zulu diplomacy, it reinforces a common stereotype of African irrationality and superstition.

There are other minor errors which Haggard might well have avoided by more careful research among readily available materials. In *Marie*, he ascribes the success of a Boer raiding expedition against

Chief Sikonyela to superior weaponry (238). In fact, the Trekkers kidnapped and bound the chief, refusing to release him until a certain number of cattle were produced. In *Child of Storm*, the final rupture between Cetshwayo and Mbulazi occurs as the result of a fight between subalterns. Cetshwayo himself said that a dance competition sparked off the war—a far more interesting explanation which Haggard might have made much of if he had spent more time going through old notes and magazines.[12] His portrayals of the Zulu kings contain a mixture of flaws and virtues. In *Marie* Dingane is absurdly shown as a capricious tyrant who lusted after white women:

with one of those almost infantile changes of mood which are common to savages of every degree he passed from wrath to laughter.

"You are quick as a lizard," he said. "Why should I, who have so many wives, want one more, who would certainly hate me? Just because she is white, and would make the others, who are black, jealous, I suppose. . . . But look you, little lizard, although you escape me between the stones, I will pull off your tail. I have said that I want to pluck this tall white flower of yours, and I will pluck her. I know where she dwells. Yes, just where the wagon she sleeps in stands in the line, for my spies have told me and I will give orders that whoever is killed, she is to be spared and brought to me living. . . ."

Now, at these ominous words, that might mean so much or so little, the sweat started to my brow and a shiver went down my back. (270—71)

Balancing that conventional black rape fantasy is a more judicious appraisal of Dingane's successor Mpande. Until recently that king has been dismissed by historians as a weak-minded buffoon. Haggard in contrast depicts him as wise and merciful. His settlement of a difficult criminal case seems to Allan Quatermain, in *Child of Storm*, to be "well reasoned and just, very different indeed from what would have been given by Dingaan or Chaka, who were wont, on less evidence, to make a clean sweep not only of the accused, but of all his family and dependents" (200). Cetshwayo, who appears in *Child of Storm* as cruel in comparison to Mbulazi, is shown in a far more favorable light in *Finished*. Instead of a warmonger anxious to "wash his spears" in combat with the British, he is portrayed as a restraining influence: "It is long since there has been a war in the land," he tells Quatermain, "and some of these young soldiers who have never used an assegai save to skin an ox or cut the head from a chicken, shout too loud and leap too high" (173).

The chief merit of these romances is not their historical veracity, which is slight. It is the wonderful ordinariness of the Zulu characters that Haggard creates, an ordinariness rarely found in the popular literature of an exceptionally racist era. His early fiction had focused on Englishmen who stripped away their veneer of civilization and entered into savage life. The later works imbue Zulu people with the motives and passions to be found in a European drawing room. Haggard seems to have been aware of this subtle, but very important shift in emphasis. In *Child of Storm* Allan Quatermain does not deliver his stock speech on the "nineteen savage parts" concealed beneath the veneer of civilization. He says this instead:

> Impossible, the clever critic will say—impossible that a savage could act with such finish. Well, friend critic, that is just where you are wrong. When you come to add it up there's very little difference in all main and essential matters between the savage and yourself.
> To begin with, by what exact right do we call people like the Zulu savages? Setting aside the habit of polygamy, which after all, is common among very highly civilised peoples in the East, they have a social system not unlike our own. They have, or had, their king, their nobles, and their commons. They have an ancient and elaborate law, and a system of morality in some ways as high as our own, and certainly more generally obeyed. They have their priests and their doctors; they are strictly upright and observe the rites of hospitality.
> . . . a clever man or woman among the people whom we call savages is in all essentials very much the same as a clever man or woman anywhere else. (89-91)

So Mameena is given the brains as well as the beauty of the Greek Helen. Her first lover is a young man of burning ambition who faces Stendhal's choice between the Red and the Black, either "the Road of Medicine" or "the Road of Spears." When, as a soldier, he achieves a high position in the Zulu court, "it was much as though some penniless country gentleman in England had been promoted in that short space of time to be one of the premier peers of the kingdom and endowed with great offices and estates" (186). At the court, people chat, plot, nurture their children, and carry on their love affairs exactly as people did in Haggard's England—and exactly as people did in his own "realistic" novels.

For this very reason, the psychodrama of the early romances, which had captivated late-Victorians struggling to come to terms with their own internal savage selves, is absent from the Zulu trilogy. Much of the gore is gone too, along with ghost wolves and cackling old materialists. Their place has been taken by people struggling for power, striving to regain lost estates, seeking exquisite revenges, and entangling themselves in love triangles which endure beyond the grave. In short, the obsessive concerns of Haggard's unsuccessful fiction have invaded Zululand as well as the other kingdoms of his imagination. The same is true of the character of Allan Quatermain, who appears to have undergone a total personality change in the later novels.

The Strange Career of Allan Quatermain

In *King Solomon's Mines* Allan Quatermain introduced himself as a rustic hunter, fifty-five years of age and totally devoted to his son who was then studying medicine in England. He was barely literate and knew only a handful of books. He had been a poor itinerant hunter-trader all his life. He had very little knowledge or experience of women. When he next appeared in the romance that bore his own name he was essentially the same man. But in later books he underwent peculiar transformations. The novelette *Allan's Wife*(1889) explained how he had fathered a son. Deep in the interior of South Africa he met a ruined English squire and fell in love with his lovely daughter Stella. She died in childbirth not long after Allan had rescued her from a pack of baboons. It was twenty years before Haggard wrote another Quatermain story. When he did, he revealed that the wily old hunter knew a great deal more about women than he could have learned in the course of his brief marriage to Stella. In fact, she was not even his first wife. As a teenager he had married the Boer girl Marie Marais. After Stella's death he had a passionate and delirious few hours of love with Mameena, "the Zulu Helen." In *Finished* he confesses that he has a special interest in studying the "burnt fingers" of people who have had unhappy love affairs. The old Zulu dwarf who sends him off in search of She warns him that "although you are so fond of women, be careful not to fall in love with that white Queen, because it would make others jealous." He has acquired a great reputation as a womanizer. Perhaps for this reason, he is not at all discomfited in *The Ancient Allan* when he is invited for a cosy weekend alone with a ravishing young widow Lady Ragnall. This story, supposed to occur only a year or two before the expedition to *King Solomon's Mines,* begins with Allan seated on a sofa next to Lady Ragnall in her private museum of Egyptian antiquities. The servants have been instructed not to disturb them. Lady

Ragnall is wearing a transparent dress. They smoke a variety of hashish called *taduki* and dream of a time when they were lovers in the days of the pharaohs.

At home in country houses with drugs and sex, this is not the Allan Quatermain that the fourteen-year-old Winston Churchill wished to hear more of in 1888.[13] And this was not the only respect in which he changed. In *Finished,* the sometime scourge of every species of African wildlife expresses a distaste for killing buffalo on the ground that "they must love life as much as we do." He disapproves of drinking and gambling. He has a "spiritual longing" to communicate with the dead.

No literary objective is served by these alterations in Allan's character. Haggard did not even make much of an effort to achieve verisimilitude in the chronology of Allan's life. The hunter had given his age as "fifty-five last birthday" in *King Solomon's Mines.* Haggard altered this figure by at least ten years in order to make Allan a witness to the Great Trek of 1836. An impossible number of adventures are set in the period 1875—86, some of which require Quatermain to be different places at the same time. The development that does occur in the character detracts rather than adds to his effectiveness. As the embodiment of pragmatism and common sense, a crusty old hunter made a perfect foil for outrageously improbable events. He represented skeptical Everyman. Fantastic happenings were more believable because he narrated them. The Allan of the later romances with his "spiritual longings," his previous existences, his country house weekends and numerous lady friends cannot fulfill that function.

Once again it can be seen that the failings of the later romances are not the consequence of a "mechanical repetition" of Haggard's early successes. They are a consequence of his departure from the formula of those successes. In his autobiography Haggard wrote that Allan was "only myself set in a variety of imagined situations, thinking my thoughts and looking at life through my eyes." That was not true of the early Allan. It is true of the later characters. Longman and others had asked for more stories of Allan in the manner of *King Solomon's Mines.* What Haggard gave them were disguised stories of Rider Haggard in the manner of *Stella Fregelius.* His fiction did not decline in popularity because he lost his skill as a writer or because he became absorbed in politics and agricultural reform. It declined because, knowing that any fiction published under his name would sell, he indulged his old *idées fixes* of love triangles, family quarrels about property, and reincarnation. The "romances" took on the character of the "novels." He gave up doing what he had once done so well, dramatizing the new ideas of evolutionary anthropology and psychology which emerged in the wake of the Darwinian revolution.

Chapter Five
Haggard's Women

One of the chief paradoxes of Haggard's literary career is that he, who wrote so much about women, should be remembered today primarily as the author of adventure stories for boys. More than half of his fictional works bear a woman's name on the title page. Perplexities about his own relations with women caused him a great deal of personal grief which often spilled onto the pages of his novels. One of his modern biographers points to women as the ultimate explanation for the success of his early romances and the failure of the later ones. According to D. S. Higgins, it was Haggard's unsatisfied passion for Lilly Jackson and his desire to please his mother that inspired his best work. The decline in his powers occurred after his mother's death and after Lilly had begun to disintegrate with venereal disease.[1] Although this explanation begs the question by failing to identify the precise elements of "inspiration" which those women are supposed to have supplied, it underscores the importance of women in Haggard's work.

Quite apart from its bearing on his own literary career, Haggard's writing about women is significant as a pointer to late-Victorian shifts in attitude toward femininity and feminism. He wrote about strong female characters at a time when people were remarking upon the emergence of "the New Woman." He created dazzling embodiments of feminine power at a time when other artists, the philosopher Nietzsche, the playwright Strindberg, and the painter Edvard Munch were depicting powerful women as vampires who suck the life out of men and whose baneful influence must be overcome. In *She*, he created a vision of womanhood which struck more powerful intellects—Andrew Lang, Sigmund Freud, and C. G. Jung—as a quintessential portrait of "the Eternal Feminine." In this chapter, Haggard's ambiguous messages about woman's role are decoded and analyzed. An attempt is made to explain why Haggard was drawn to powerful women but recoiled from feminism. The chapter closes by asking the question, "who was *She?*"

Haggard's Frankness about Relations Between Men and Women

Both the novels and the romances bear ample witness to Haggard's dictum that "sexual passion lies at the root of all things human." His very first work of fiction, *Dawn,* had tackled, more or less head on, the topics of adultery and sex outside of marriage. *Colonel Quaritch, V.C.* and *Joan Haste* touched on the question of prostitution. And even the romances, which introduced various sorts of sexual deviation in disguised form, were surprisingly open about sex. His comical novel *Mr. Meeson's Will* presents the passenger steamer as "Cupid's own hot-bed." Ustane's seduction of Leo Vincey in *She* is candidly justified on the ground that roses must be gathered while they may. "And now," she implores him, "let us love and take that which is given us, and be happy; for in the grave there is no love and no warmth, nor any touching of the lips. . . . To-night the hours are our own; how know we to whom they shall belong tomorrow." There is also an astonishing amount of female nudity in the romances. Before Ayesha's final naked dance into the eternal fire she has disrobed half-a-dozen times with stunning effects on her male admirers: "and as she stood the white robe slipped from her down to her golden girdle, baring the blinding loveliness of her form." Mameena, "the Zulu Helen," not only possesses the figure of a Greek statue, her costume, "except for her little bead apron and a single string of large blue beads about her throat", was "well, that of a Greek statue." *People of the Mist* verges on the pornographic in the slave camp scene when the brutal commandant shouts, "Here, let men see what they are going to buy, and gripping the breast of her white robe he rent it open."

There are three remarkable features in Haggard's candid treatment of sexuality. First, he got away with it in an age that is still celebrated for its suppression of sex in all its forms. Second, one of his favorite themes is role reversal in male-female relations. Women are cast as rulers and high priests. They take the initiative in romance. Some of Haggard's imaginary exotic societies are matriarchal and matrilineal. Third, he nevertheless maintained a steady opposition to feminism both as a movement and as an ideal. How is this last aspect of his treatment of women to be reconciled with the first two? The place to begin is with his strong female characters.

Profiles of Powerful Women

There are some ugly, evil women (Hendrika the baboon lady and Gagool) in Haggard's gallery of strong feminine personalities, but for the most part they epitomize beauty. He avoids altogether the conventional male aspersions cast on clever women, that they are mannish or plain. Mameena is a perfect copy of a statue. "The might of Cleopatra's beauty lay" in "a glory and a radiance cast through the fleshly covering from the fierce soul within." Ayesha could, when she chose, cast aside her instruments of power and stand forth as "an incarnation of lovely, tempting womanhood, made more perfect—and in a way more spiritual—than ever woman was before her."

Yet for all their irresistible physical appeal, these women all betray, in some way or another, a flaw in the overall perfection. That flaw is the massive brain power that lurks behind their radiant visages. With Mameena "there was something not quite pleasing about that beautiful face; something, notwithstanding its childlike outline, which reminded me of a flower breaking into bloom, that one does not associate with youth and innocence. I tried to analyze what this might be, and came to the conclusion that without being hard, it was too clever and, in a sense, too reflective." The "brain within the shapely head was keen and bright as polished steel . . . this woman was one made to rule, not to be man's toy, or even his loving companion, but to use him for her ends." In Ayesha's eyes one sees "the very diablerie of the woman," which, "whilst it horrified and repelled, attracted in an even greater degree." That fatal something was the product of her overwhelming combination of extraordinary intelligence with "the experience of two thousand years."

Haggard frequently attributes this fatal combination of beauty and brains to associations with powers of darkness. Many of these women wear golden snakes as their only item of jewelry, snakes that simultaneously suggest Satan the tempter of Eve and Eve the tempter of Adam. Meriamun, the villain of *The World's Desire*, can call her snake to life at will. "Greater it grew and greater yet, and as it grew it shone like a torch in a tomb, and wound itself about the body of Meriamun, wrapping her in its fiery folds till it reached her middle. Then it reared its head on high . . . and lo! its face was the face of a fair woman—it was the face of Meriamun." Swanhild in *Eric Brighteyes* traffics with the devil in the form of a female toad. Ayesha presides over convocations of ghastly fiends from Hell. In every case there is the suggestion that the association of physical loveliness and intellect is unnatural in women. Cleopatra's peculiarity is that there was met in her "all the splendors that have been given to woman for her glory, and all the genius which man has won from heaven." That is to say, genius in men comes from heaven; genius in women comes from hell.

Genius in action for Haggard's women means immoral methods employed to achieve amoral ends. Cleopatra embodies "evil of that greater sort, which fearing nothing, and making a mock of laws, has taken empires for its place of play." Lady Bellamy, "the spirit of power" in *Dawn,* employs vice as a conscious instrument of her ambition, proclaiming that "it is by their vices, properly managed, that women always have risen, and always will rise." Swanhild's only joy aside from the pursuit of raw power is "to make a sport of men and put them to shame and grief." Ayesha preaches the irrelevance of religion and the pleasures of despotic rule.

"Good" Women

And yet Haggard's heroines do not lack brains. In order to tease out his essential message about women and their proper role in society it is necessary to set "good" women along side the bad women and to compare them. This was something Haggard himself was fond of doing. His first novel, *Dawn,* contrasted the characters of Angela and Lady Bellamy. *The Witch's Head* drew a similar contrast between Florence and Eva Ceswick. In the early romances he sharpened and stylized these contrasts. Ustane is paired with Ayesha in *She,* Nyleptha with Sorais in *Allan Quatermain,* Helen with Meriamun in *The World's Desire,* and Gudruda with Swanhild in *Eric Brighteyes.* The list could be extended to a great length. In physical appearance there is little to differentiate between the contrasted pairs. All are beautiful. All have eyes of grey or "cyprian violet." Small external characteristics, however, indicate the moral distinctions between them. The "good women" are generally blondes. The bad ones are brunettes. They also have longer hair, in some cases suggesting the Magdalene of medieval legend. So, while Nylephtha's golden hair clusters in "short ringlets" about the head, Sorais her twin sister, has "coal-black" hair which falls "in masses on her shoulders." Gudruda's golden hair reaches her arms, but her rival Swanhild possesses enough brown hair "to veil her to the knees."

Haggard distinguishes much more strikingly between the uses to which the good and bad women apply their physical charms. The bad women unscrupulously employ their bodies to gain their objectives of love, wealth, and power. Ayesha is a creature of a thousand moods and is capable of choosing any one of them to suit the occasion at hand. "A new mood was on her," Haggard writes, "and the color of her fathomless mind had changed beneath it. It was no longer torture-torn and hateful, as I had seen it when she was cursing her dead rival by the leaping flames, no longer icily terrible as in the judgement-hall; no longer rich, and somber, and splendid . . . as in the dwellings of the dead. No, her mood now was that of Aphrodite triumphing." She can blow a "fragrant breath" on Horace Holly which makes him suddenly lose control of his passions. And she can just as easily emanate invisible vibrations which chill him "back to common sense, and a knowledge of propriety and the domestic virtues." She and all the other amoral women dress and undress to produce calculated effects on the men they dominate.

The good women, on the other hand, modestly and deliberately refrain from unleashing the full force of their physical and mental faculties. In *The World's Desire,* Helen catches her rival Meriamun using magic to lure Odysseus, but refuses to retaliate in kind, "for never shall Helen work by shameful guile or magic." Nyleptha always dresses more modestly than her cold-hearted sister, and thereby achieves a more perfect loveliness, "for beauty, dependant as it is to a certain extent upon the imagination, is never so beautiful as when it is half hid." When Eric Brighteyes sees Gudruda bathing in a pond, he is caught up in a passion which totally eclipses the rival attractions of Swanhild. Nevertheless Gudruda hurriedly throws a cloak round herself and berates him for sneaking up on her. She will not use her body to win him.

Thus all the contrasted pairs of women point up the same lesson, that is, that the best women are those who let their greatest powers lie dormant, who suppress their sexuality and whose finest hours come when they sacrifice themselves for their men and their children.

Haggard and Feminism

His insistence on that point stood as the one insurmountable obstacle to his acceptance of the doctrines espoused by the "New Women" and feminists of his age. He had no difficulty in acknowledging women as social and intellectual equals. His own mother was an example of literary talent and ambition hampered by motherhood and an anti-intellectual husband. Early in his career he recognized the greatness of Olive Schreiner and sought her friendship.[2] During his most creative period he relied for literary advice as

much on his secretary Agnes Barber as he did on his famous friend
Andrew Lang.[3] Despite his hankering after fantasms of romance,
Haggard was not good at flirtation. He preferred debating with clever
women to conventional gallantries. His nephew recalled that "Rider
had no small talk with women, and when he found things were not
going well, then he became gauche and got himself disliked. Any
woman who stood up to him he took to at once. The pair were soon at
it hammer and tongs."[4] It was not because he was an easy target that
the feminist Lady Florence Dixie wrote to him to complain about the
treatment of women in *Beatrice*. It was because he stood apart from
the general run of males in his willingness to acknowledge woman's
capacity for deep thought, political acumen, and physical bravery.

This aspect of late-Victorian feminism is set out at length in both
his realistic novels and his exotic romances. The heroine of his first
novel *Dawn* is a woman of exceptional intelligence and scholarship, so
exceptional, in fact, that she is generally regarded as a freak. One conventional gentleman explains to her condescendingly that "both
history and observation teach us that great gifts like yours partake of
the character of an accident in a woman; they are not natural to her."
If "a woman had all the genius of Plato or all the learning of
Solomon, it would be forgotten at the touch of a baby's fingers."
This was not Haggard's own opinion. He toyed with the idea of
writing a sequel to *Dawn* in which he would show Angela "after a
spell of ordinary married life and becoming the mother of a charming
family [,] falling again under the fascination of her love of knowledge
and power and unable to any longer keep in check the mighty intellect now only beginning to touch its possibilities."[5]

She and Haggard's other early heroines keenly appreciate—and
resent—the social conventions which confine their talents. In addition
to Jess who dreams in her South African home of conquering the pin-
nacles of European fame, there is Beatrice whose only outlet for ambition is to promote the career of her married lover. She tells him frankly that while he can realistically work toward writing his name into the
history books, "women have no future and they ask none. At least I
do not now, though once I did. It is enough for them if they can ever
so little help the lives of others. That is their happiness and their
reward is—rest." Haggard portrays in grim, convincing prose the fate
of women who cannot find or accept that subordinated, sacrificial role
in life: the Ceswick sisters whose lonely, dangerous position as orphaned spinsters spurs them into a jealous competition for the love of
potential male protectors; Joan Haste who must submit herself to pet-

ty tyranny and sexual harassment as a department store fashion model; Ida de la Molle, Angela Caresfoot, Ellen Graves, and a score of others who regretfully or cynically "sell" themselves in marriage to men they do not love in order to advance the fortunes of their impoverished families. (This latter practice Haggard frequently compared to bridewealth exchanges of women for cattle among the Zulu.)

In the romances, where he was unconfined by the requirements of verisimilitude and free to explore a wider range of social situations, Haggard made even stronger comments on feminism. He could explore the theoretically possible range of male-female relationships by standing Victorian conventions on their head. Some of the new evolutionary anthropologists with whom he and Andrew Lang were so well in tune, raised the speculative possibility that the human race had once passed through a matriarchal stage. The opening, pseudo-anthropological scenes of life among the "Amahagger" in *She* work out some of the implications of a society where "individuals are as proud of a long and superior female ancestry as we are of our families in Europe," while male parenthood is not even acknowledged. Haggard's mouthpiece Holly certifies that "there is nothing immoral about this Amahagger custom" which the people accepted "much as we accept the income tax or our marriage laws." Haggard subjects his woman-hating manservant Job to a Gilbertian sexual attack from an overripe, overweight Amahagger. He also has an old man remark that every second generation or so the men find their subordination unbearable, whereupon they "rise, and kill the old ones [women] as an example to the young ones, and to show them that we are the strongest." Nevertheless, this and other similar passages in the early romances are valid evidence of Haggard's acknowledgment that the social positions of men and women were fixed by convention rather than nature.

The strong women of the romances vehemently denounce this situation and refuse to conform to customs which would enslave them. Cleopatra nourishes a particular hatred for wedlock: "the worst slavery of our sex." Grown women, she explains, have "two ills to fear—Death and Marriage; and of these twain is Marriage the more vile; for in Death we may find rest, but in Marriage, should it fail us, we must find hell." Mameena, Haggard's irresistible Zulu, delivers an impassioned tirade against men in general when the last of her schemes has collapsed. "You men weary me, as men have always done, being but fools whom it is so easy to make drunk, and who when drunk are so unpleasing. *Piff!* I am tired of you sober and cunning, and I am tired of you drunken and brutal.''

Such extreme denunciations raise the specter of female self-
sufficiency. Haggard toys fearfully with this concept in many of the
romances, beginning with *Allan's Wife* (1889). Hendrika, a white
woman raised by baboons, competes ferociously with Allan Quatermain for the love of Stella Carson. She affirms that woman's love for
woman surpasses heterosexual love in passion and fidelity. She kid-
naps Stella to prevent her from bearing Allan's children. Haggard,
speaking through Quatermain, expounds an interesting Darwinist explanation for Hendrika's fanatical jealousy. Although "it is generally
supposed that this passion only exists in strength when the object loved is of another sex from the lover,'' his experience leads him to
believe otherwise. The "lower one gets in the scale of humanity, the
more readily this passion thrives; indeed, it may be said to come to its
intensest perfection in brutes. Women are more jealous than those of
larger mind and wider sympathy, and animals are the most jealous of
all.'' Hendrika acts as she does because she was "not far removed
from animals.'' This passage is remarkable as an extremely rare example of Haggard appearing to place women below men on the evolutionary ladder. It is also remarkable as a frank recognition of intense
female sexuality at a time when medical men and feminists alike were
inclined to ignore it.

In chapter 3, Haggard's accounts of homosexual attachments were
presented as examples of the way in which the romance provided a
"safe" arena where late-Victorian readers could approach subjects
which were ordinarily taboo. In the context of Haggard's analysis of
woman's role, they stand as a revealing glimpse of one perceptive
male's anxieties in an era when legal and social restraints on women
were beginning to loosen. What if women did not need men at all?
What if they secretly despised them as Mameena did? What if they
could get along on their own, as Hendrika insisted? The man-hating,
celibate female companion recurs often in Haggard's later romances.
Soa in *People of the Mist*, Sihamba in *Swallow*, Nombé in *Finished*
and Nehushta in *Pearl Maiden* are all examples—some good and
some wicked—of strong, clever females who have renounced
heterosexual love and whose sole object in life is to serve an adored
woman.

Occasionally Haggard writes horrific accounts of women acting
together in unmitigated opposition to men. At the climax of
Montezuma's Daughter when the Indian armies have been
decimated by the final Spanish assault upon their mountain fortress,

the women secretly plan and carry through an orgy of human sacrifice. They rip the hearts from the breasts of men in a scene which Haggard likens to the mad rites of Euripides' Bacchae. A more overtly political instance of women's solidarity appears in *The World's Desire,* the underrated romance which Haggard wrote with Andrew Lang. The strongest possible contrast is drawn between Helen of Troy and the Egyptian Queen Meriamun whose conflict is the central subject of the book. Although both women seek love and power through their control of men, they employ different weapons. Meriamun uses magic, brute force, cunning, and her body. Helen cultivates a mystique which drives men mad by playing upon their unfulfillable dreams of ideal womanhood. Protected by ghostly swordsmen in her temple of beauty, she tantalizes and teases men with her siren song.

> Ye that seek me, ye that sue me,
>   Ye that flock beneath my tower,
> Ye would win me, would undo me,
>   I must perish in an hour,
> Dead before the Love that slew me, clasped the
>   Bride and crushed the flower.
> Hear the word and mark the warning,
>   Beauty lives but in your sight,
> Beauty fades from all men's scorning
>   In the watches of the night,
> Beauty wanes before the morning, and
>   Love dies in his delight.

This double-barreled message, that men do not desire real women but thirst after phantasmagorical images of their own making, and that they soon despise the women they conquer, does not abate the ardor of the men who listen. "A moan of desire" rises from the milling crowd which surges forward in a suicidal frenzy. One by one they are swiftly cut down by the swords of Helen's invisible guardians. Meriamun responds to Helen's taunts by raising an army of women to storm the temple. With a war cry of "Arise, my sisters!" she calls upon them to avenge their dead husbands, sons, and brothers by striking at the cause of their affliction. That cause is not the physical Helen, but the concept of womanhood she represents. So long as men bow down before the pedestal of an unrealistic, unattainable ideal, they will despise the real women they keep as wives and lovers. So long, too, will they brutalize and seduce them and be unfaithful to them.

This is among the most striking of the images of women which coexisted in the minds of European men at the end of the last century. Threatened men like Nietzsche conceived woman as vampire. Liberal individualists like Ibsen perceived woman as the prisoners of a "doll's house" whose door would open if they dared. Haggard reasoned that the feminine mystique was as great an obstacle to the emancipation of women as social convention, unfair laws, and mistaken theories of mental inferiority. The reason that he could not mount a public platform to denounce the mystique was that he believed it to be a permanent fixture of male imaginations. Therefore no feminist crusade could ever succeed in stamping it out. Haggard's antifeminism thus arose from three sources. The first was his instinctive feeling that it was immoral for women to use their brains as men used their brains and to pursue power as men pursued power. The second was his anxiety about the social consequences of women achieving self-sufficiency either alone or in groups. The third was his belief that male fantasies of ideal womanhood were ingrained in human nature. He offered no practical solutions to the disabilities of women in his own society—disabilities of which he was keenly aware.[6] He retreated instead to hopes of a better life beyond the grave when the schism between the male and female parts of the human soul should finally be healed.

Who Was "She"?

Haggard's literary friends and foes alike proclaimed his Ayesha, "She-Who-Must-Be-Obeyed," to be an astoundingly original creation. She took the world by storm in the 1880s and continues to captivate new readers today. In contrast to *King Solomon's Mines,* which drew on a number of readily identifiable sources from Haggard's reading and his South African experiences, there are very few clues to the origins of *She.* Haggard himself could not explain how he had created her. In his autobiography he recalled that, when he sat down to write, his "ideas as to its development were of the vaguest. The only clear notion that I had in my head was that of an immortal woman inspired by an immortal love. All the rest shaped itself round this figure. And it came—it came faster than my poor aching hand could set it down." Apart from this theory of spontaneous creation Haggard offers only one other scrap of evidence. The name She-Who-Must-Be-Obeyed came originally from a rag doll with which the family nurse used to terrify his brothers and sisters into obedience.[7] Haggard's daughter claimed that it was young Rider himself who was terrified of the doll.[8]

Morton Cohen's biographical study of Haggard speculates extensively on the origins and meaning of She without coming to any firm conclusions.[9] Haggard certainly knew by 1896, and may have known before, of rumors which circulated concerning light-skinned magician-queens of the Lovedu people in the northeastern Transvaal.[10] There is a vague kinship between his heroine and other beautiful, vengeful characters in late-Victorian fiction. But Ayesha's longevity amounting to immortality, her towering intellect, and her ability to reveal genuine tenderness as well as implacable passion have no close equivalents either in African legends or English literature. Students of myth and the psyche have suggested other explanations of her significance. Freud saw her as the embodiment of "the Eternal Feminine," a somewhat nebulous idea of early German romanticism.[11] Carl Jung's idea of the anima is closely allied to this notion. Jung's anima is the ideal image of womanhood which a man projects upon the female object of his affection. The love he believes he feels for her is in reality his devotion to an interior ideal inherited from the racial memories of his ancestors. Haggard would have had no difficulty in subscribing to Jung's analysis. He and Lang embodied a practically identical doctrine in the allegorical figure of Helen which they concocted in *The World's Desire*.[12] (Here again psychoanalytic theory is reflected rather than proved in Haggard's fiction.)

But if Ayesha is meant to personify an unattainable dream of femininity, how are her less endearing traits to be explained? Are cruelty, homicide, jealousy, atheism, and an insatiable drive for power features of ideal womanhood? Would a late-Victorian version of that ideal have been adept, as Ayesha was, at chemistry and biology? She shares some characteristics of Haggard's anemic heroines, but she shares other characteristics with his villains. When she shrivels up after her reentry into the sacred fire, she changes form and stature. First she shrinks to the size and general appearance of "a badly preserved Egyptian mummy." Then she turns simian. " 'Look!' shrieked Job. . . . 'she's turning into a monkey.' " At the time Haggard wrote *She* he had not yet created Hendrika the baboon lady, but he had created the witch Gagool who is repeatedly likened to a monkey. At her first appearance in *King Solomon's Mines* she is mistaken for "a withered-up monkey, wrapped in a fur coat." Later "the wizened monkey-like creature" is revealed as "a woman of great age so shrunken that in size it seemed no larger than the face of a year-old child.'' Like Ayesha, Gagool is immensely old and like her, she believes that power and self-gratification are alone worth seeking in a godless universe. The climax of *She* discloses that inside the visage of radiant beauty which Ayesha acquired in the sacred fire, she was the very image of Gagool.

Much significance also lurks in the Egyptian mummy stage which Ayesha passes through before she becomes a monkey. Haggard portrays Ayesha's capital of Kor as the "mother of Egyptian civilization." Early in the story he speculated with a frankly prurient interest on the bygone love lives of the attractive mummies who are preserved in the caves beneath the city.[13] The same idea is explored in his short story "Smith and the Pharaohs" which describes the results of a bank clerk's infatuation with the mummy of a pharaoh's wife. Both Ayesha and the mummy are sexually desired but rendered forever unattainable by age and death.

D. S. Higgins has argued that Haggard's use of the monkey, an ancient symbol of wickedness and lust, and Ayesha's destruction by fire are evidence that repressed sexual desire is the underlying theme of *She*. According to Higgins, Haggard's continued longing for the lost love of his youth, his unsatisfactory marriage, and his guilt over a sexual escapade in South Africa were unconsciously expressed in the story of a woman who turns into a repulsive hag at the moment before her promised physical union with her lover.[14] In other words, Haggard desired sex but was so consumed with guilt that he recoiled with disgust at the prospect of actual physical contact. The trouble with this psychological theory is that it does not accord with the rest of Haggard's life and work. Could the man who joked, "Holy Mother, thus believing, may we sin without conceiving," who wrote novels about prostitution, bigamy, and adultery, who affirmed that "sexual passion lies at the root of all things human"—could such a man be fairly described as repressed where ordinary heterosexual relations were concerned?

Yet, if Higgins did not arrive at a convincing answer in his search for She, he may have been on the right track. There is a case to make for Ayesha as the disguised embodiment of an unfulfilled desire for a forbidden love, a son's incestuous longing for his mother.[15] Haggard's novels deal candidly with the tensions hidden in the bosoms of Victorian families. Fierce sibling rivalries pit brother against brother in battle, sister against sister in love affairs. Sons are rejected by their fathers and struggle to displace them. Haggard's own father is drawn from life in several novels as a wild, blustering, unreasonable squire of the old school. Haggard frequently writes of love between children who have been raised "as brother and sister." In *Nada the Lily* the suggestion of sibling incest is made even stronger; Umslopogaas and Nada really believe themselves to be brother and sister. The only member of the family ignored in Haggard's fiction is mother.

She simply is not there. Angela's mother died in childbirth, as did Leo Vincey's and Gudruda's. The mothers of Umslopogaas, Jess, Ida de la Molle, Arthur Heigham, the Pearl Maiden, the Ceswick Sisters, Stella Carson, Morris Monk, and Allan Quatermain are all dead. When mothers do appear they are usually quickly hustled off the stage. Thomas Wingfield's mother is killed off in the first chapter of *Montezuma's Daughter.* Eric Brighteyes' aged mother is briefly introduced and then forgotten. Only in the later novels *Joan Haste* (1895) and *The Ancient Allan* (1920) do any mothers take any part in the action without dying. The almost total absence of mothers in the works of a writer so prolific as Rider Haggard demands some explanation.

Ayesha can be interpreted as a mother in disguise. She is an older woman who is all-powerful, wise, and knowing. She is totally devoted to the young object of her affection. She will do anything—murder, plunder, or destroy—to advance his interests. She will not allow any young woman to take him away from her. Thus far she accords well with many a young man's perceptions of a dominating mother. The element of fantasy enters when she holds out the prospect of marriage. She has kept her youthful beauty in order to win him. She has waited for him to grow up and come to her. But at the last moment she shrivels up and dies. Nature and Fate have thrown up impossible barriers to their physical union. In the sequel, *The Return of She,* Ayesha is cast as the head priestess of a cult whose central symbol is an idealized representation of Universal Motherhood.

This interpretation of Ayesha's character is in keeping with what little is known about Haggard's early life and his attitudes toward his mother. The rag doll of the nursery named She-Who-Must-Be-Obeyed calls to mind the mother who ruled that domain as an absolute monarch. By taking up literature, Haggard was following in her footsteps. He had her literary testament published at his own expense. *Cleopatra,* the book which most closely resembles *She* in its delineation of a strong, irresistible female character, was the romance he chose to dedicate to her. He still "could not bear" to write of her death more than twenty years after she had gone.[16]

Many taboos have fallen in the last hundred years but even in the permissive atmosphere of the late twentieth century the subject of incest retains its ability to shock. So does Haggard's Ayesha who remains the most durably popular of all his characters. It may not be too farfetched to suggest that succeeding generations of readers experience the same mixture of fascination and terror that Victorians felt because they grasp the same subliminal significance in the tale of a young man's impossible love for an old woman.

The subject merits closer study as does almost everything Rider Haggard wrote about women. Whatever his defects as a literary craftsman, he explored a greater range of important questions concerning woman's sexuality and woman's role in a male dominated society than almost any male author of his time.

Chapter Six
Haggard's Politics
Haggard's Imperialism: For and Against

Nothing has annoyed Rider Haggard's admirers more than the charge frequently leveled against him that his fiction celebrated the imperialism which was rampant in Britain at the close of the nineteenth century. In one form or another this indictment has dogged his reputation since the days of his first success. He was called "the novelist of Blood." It was said that his work, like the work of his friend Rudyard Kipling, marked an unfortunate watershed in British literary history. It appealed to "the young Englishman" who, tired of psychological complications in literature, "longed to go out and shoot something he could understand."[1] Because his novels of African adventure appeared at the same time that European powers were scrambling for Africa, it has been suggested that he somehow helped to provoke the scramble. "Imperialist indoctrination of the young," writes G. N. Sanderson, was not "confined to the hours of formal instruction. Rider Haggard and the *Boy's Own Paper* saw to that."[2] Critics denigrate him as a simple-minded "defender of the flag" and as a spokesman for the poisonous doctrines of racism which the budding science of anthropology was developing in the same era.[3]

Haggard's defenders can cite a great deal of contrary evidence. Very little of the imperialism which Haggard preached from public platforms and in the press is written into his romances. Not one of them describes a colonial war or a territorial annexation. He does not take his readers, as did his contemporary G. A. Henty, "with Clive to India" or "with Kitchener to Khartoum." Haggard's "savages" are the best and cleverest to appear in novels since James Fenimore Cooper's Mohicans. Alan Sandison contends that in *King Solomon's Mines,* as in every other book he wrote on Africa, "he repudiates without fuss, the whole arrogant notion of the white man's burden."[4] No adolescent is known to have been inspired to build empires by reading Haggard's books. The British Empire had already ballooned outward to its furthest frontiers by the time those young men grew up and achieved positions of responsibility.

Another line of defense has been to try and dissociate Haggard
from the rest of the loose-knit company of imperialist writers. Kipling
may well have been a jingo and a racist, so may have been G. A. Henty and John Buchan. But Haggard was different. At least so the argument goes. P. B. Ellis claims that "he demonstrated in his books that
the British Empire was, to him, a thing of transience as had been all
the other empires since the dawn of time." Moreover, "when Haggard came up against a *genuine* imperialist, the man for whom empire spelled financial exploitation and profit, he was sickened."[5] In a
not dissimilar vein, Morton Cohen seizes on Haggard's support for
government interference in agriculture as evidence that he was,
"whether he recognized it or not, a radical-socialist."[6] D. S. Higgins
represents Haggard as unsympathetic to the British side in the Boer
War.[7] The apparent purpose of such arguments is to disentangle Haggard from imperialism because the word stinks in the nostrils of
modern sensibilities. The parallel effort to play down his associations
with the Conservative party seems to be motivated by a desire to make
him more acceptable to literary people who are generally disinclined
to favor the political right.

These well-meant efforts to clean up Haggard's politics are unnecessary, misinformed, and deceptive. Unnecessary because literary
quality is not the monopoly of any particular political faction; able
writers have attached themselves at various times to liberal, conservative, fascist, and communist movements. Dissociating Haggard
from Tory imperialism on the ground that he was known to favor
state interference in the economy is misinformed because it identifies
conservatism with laissez-faire capitalism, and thereby seriously
misreads the character of "the New Imperialism" at the turn of the
century. Insisting that Haggard was a closet radical or a socialist
unawares is misleading because it directs attention away from the important and subtle interplay of political and nonpolitical ideas in his
fiction. In the remainder of this chapter his political ideas and affilia-
tions are summarized. The reasons why some of them were written into his romances and some were not are explored. Finally, a brief set of
speculations on the probable political implications and effects of his
writings is presented.

"Rank Jingoism"

If the world had no novels or romances by Rider Haggard, the
evidence demonstrating his adulation of the British Empire presented

by his speeches, articles, and letters to the press would have to be judged overwhelming and incontrovertible. Shortly after Cecil Rhodes's British South Africa Company had obliterated the armies of the independent African king Lobengula in "Rhodesia," Haggard told the Anglo-African Writers' Club that he had "followed the track of the invading columns in Matabeleland with pride and sympathy." As for Lobengula's admittedly brave soldiers, "well, their hour had come, and they had to go, taking with them their cruelties and superstitions," so that the Pax Britannica might be established "beneath whose aegis their children and their brothers might dwell in quietness." In the same speech he affirmed that it was "for our good, for the good of the Empire, and of the world at large, that Englishmen with English traditions, and ideas should dominate in Africa." Some, he knew, would call this attitude vulgar. "That was rank Jingoism—his sin was ever before him: but all the same while he had a voice to speak, a pen to write, or any power to move the hearts of men, he meant to go on sinning thus, for to him the English name was the most glorious in history, and the English flag the most splendid that ever flew above the peoples of the earth."[8]

That extraordinary speech was no momentary aberration. Nor will any Haggard speech support Sandison's claim that he repudiated "the whole arrogant notion of the white man's burden." On the contrary, he was a special friend to Rudyard Kipling who invented that famous phrase in 1898. While introducing Kipling at a dinner of the Anglo-African Writers' Club in that same year, Haggard affirmed his unshakable belief "in the divine right of a great civilising people—that is, in their divine mission."[9] Nowhere, he continued, could one find more eloquent expressions of that mission than in Kipling's poems, "The Song of the English" and "the English Flag." There is no evidence that Haggard ever opposed or condemned any British invasion or annexation of any territory on earth.

From his early days on Shepstone's staff in the Transvaal he maintained a steadfast conviction that it was *failure* to act, *failure* to annex, *failure* to govern firmly that caused problems for Britain overseas. When Bishop Colenso and Lady Florence Dixie raised a campaign to have Cetshwayo reinstated as king of the Zulu, Haggard predicted that the agitation would "probably succeed" because "the ex-King is big and black, and has, therefore, like Jumbo [the elephant], claims to the sympathy and consideration of English society." He also predicted (accurately) that unless all of Zululand were annexed and ruled according to Shepstone's maxims, the king's return would precipitate a ruinous civil war.[10] Likewise he never tired of predicting that the British retrocession of the Transvaal Republic would in the long run lead to a far more bloody struggle between Boer and Briton for supremacy in southern Africa. In 1883 he wrote that there remained "but one remedy, and that a very vulgar one—force."[11] He did not, as Higgins asserts, soften his attitude on the eve of the second Boer War in 1899. He told a tory rally in August of that year that the condition of white and brown British subjects in the Transvaal could "no longer be tolerated."[12] When the war came, he described it as "absolutely necessary"; it "had been forced upon them, and it must be fought to the bitter end."[13]

Speculators and missionaries are sometimes scorned in Haggard's fiction but he warmly supported them in public life. He likened the Episcopal missionaries of Central Africa to "the martyrs of old" and spurred them on in their efforts to stamp out superstition. "Men did not know," he informed a missionary fund raising dinner, "what superstition was until they had consorted with an African native." Superstition "meant that a mother would treat her child with every cruelty that they could conceive could be practiced in its name, and was daily, and to this hour practiced. Women would be burnt alive, men would be butchered; the whole world there, in short, groaned beneath this yoke of superstition."[14] Even after his short-lived involvement in South African speculative ventures, Haggard remained on excellent terms with big capitalists. In 1899 he extended warm welcomes both to the labor-recruiting freebooter Percy Fitzpatrick and to the mining magnate Lionel Phillips.[15] At the Anglo-African Writers' Club he introduced Phillips as belonging "to that class that is called capitalists. In his opinion it was, perhaps, one of the most deserving and down-trodden classes in the kingdom. . . . The capitalist was the person who did everything; in his wilder moments of generosity he even bought six-shilling novels."

It is therefore quite misleading for Ellis to write that "when Haggard came up against a *genuine* imperialist, the man for whom empire spelled financial exploitation and profit, he was sickened." Not only did he dine quite comfortably with such men before the Boer War, he maintained public support for their policies after that debacle had drawn to its ironic and heartrending end. He recommended that South Africa be flooded with British emigrants to overbalance the Boer population and that the mine owners' importation of cheap Chinese labor be allowed to continue without interference from the imperial government.[16] Although Haggard said that "he

did not like the Chinese'' and ''would rather they had not gone
there,'' the mines ''were the greatest industry, and for these they required enormous quantities of labor.'' It was said that ''white men
could work these mines but such was not the case; whilst the natives
were too well off to work much.''

Set against the background of a lifetime's commitment to imperial
expansion and the Conservative party, Haggard's later reactionary
schemes—his work for the Anti-Bolshevik league, and his plan for
''upper class inhabitants of the United Kingdom'' to escape high
taxes by moving en masse to South Africa—cannot be dismissed as
merely the follies of curmudgeonly old age.[17] Rider Haggard was not
an ideological scatterbrain. To understand the logical connections between the diverse objectives to which he was politically committed, it is
necessary to view them against the background of the ''New Imperialism'' espoused by Joseph Chamberlain and his coterie at the
turn of the century.

Imperialism and Social Reform

The ''New Imperialism'' was a slang expression coined by the press
in the 1890s. It summed up the surprise felt by the British people at
the changes which the last two decades had wrought in international
relations. In the 1860s Great Britain had been preeminent among nations, the only superpower of the age. She led the world in industrial
production. Her empire girdled the globe. Her navy was unchalleng-
ed and unchallengable. According to her most prestigious political
and economic philosophers, she was leading the world into an un-
precedented golden age of peace and free trade. Events confounded
these optimistic predictions. First America, then Germany, France,
and Japan achieved the industrial capacity required to break Britain's
stranglehold on their marketplaces. The newcomers scorned the doctrine of free trade, preferring instead to surround themselves with
high tariff walls to keep out the products of their competitors. This
trend toward national exclusiveness caused businessmen and
economists in many countries to worry about the future. Where were
they to find customers and raw materials in years to come? Increasing
attention was paid to dismal prophets who preached that only armed
force could guarantee secure futures for industrial and commercial nations, force to win new areas and to hold old ones. When Germany
embarked on a program to build a first-class navy, when the United
States went to war against Spain in two oceans, and when Japan

emerged from nowhere as a dominant power in the Far East, these predictions appeared to be coming true.

Against this background of threats and uncertainties, late-Victorian imperialism in Britain displayed a defensive state of mind. The most energetic expansionists believed that they were racing against the clock to "prepare a British empire to survive in a world of continental super-states."[18] They were inclined to believe that this required them to adopt some of the methods of their competitors. Free trade might have to go. The state would have to play a more direct role in commerce and industry. Men might have to be drafted in order to build up the armed forces. In the interests of "national efficiency," the government would need to raise the living standards of the lower classes and institute minimum standards of health and welfare. Bernard Semmel has shown in his book *Imperialism and Social Reform* that this peculiar mix of tariffs, colonialism, armaments, big government, and social welfare appealed to a wide spectrum of people ranging from landed gentry to Fabian socialists.[19] But the bulk of the enthusiasts were associated with the Conservative party and grouped themselves around the energetic figure of Joseph Chamberlain.

Rider Haggard supported Chamberlain and what he stood for. There was consequently nothing especially peculiar about his simultaneous support for big capital in South Africa, conscription in Britain, social regeneration in the cities, and state aid for agricultural reform in the countryside. The empire must, he felt, adapt to new circumstances and strain every nerve to meet threats from rival nations. However, the way Haggard expressed his commitment to the "New Imperialism" reflected his own long-standing prejudices. As the son of a squire and the proprietor of Ditchingham estate, he believed that agriculture was the backbone of England. Great statesmen, wise generals, and brave soldiers sprang naturally from the countryside. They would not grow in the crowded unhealthy cities. In plain, practical terms, it worried him that free trade had made Britain depend upon imported foodstuffs which a determined enemy might choke off in wartime. Soldiers could not be recruited from the undernourished, unfit ranks of the urban working classes. Like many others of his time, he believed that the birthrate was falling and that this presaged the decline of the Anglo-Saxon race. His preferred remedies for all these problems were to halt the decline of English agriculture and to put men back on the land.[20] If they could not be put back on the green fields of England, they could be sent out to the wide-open spaces of the colonies.

He spent much of the thirty years between his unsuccessful candidacy for parliament in 1895 and his death promoting this goal in various ways. He recognized, though he regretted, that Britain was probably too inexorably committed to free trade ever to reintroduce a comprehensive schedule of tariffs which could protect English farmers against foreign producers.[21] Nevertheless a package of mild protective measures and selective subsidies to farmers might alleviate the worst consequences of unchecked foreign competition. The state might also encourage private initiative in subdividing sections of large estates into small farms which could supplement the incomes of tradesmen and craftsmen from the city. The Garden City Movement could not of itself cure all the ills of England, but it could give many people employed in commerce and industry a semirural alternative to a debilitating existence in the established urban wastelands. Salvation Army "labor colonies" in Canada Haggard regarded as the best possible response of private benevolence to the plight of the derelict, unemployed male population of the cities.[22] His later schemes for settling ex-soldiers on farms in the underpopulated sections of the Empire were another means to the same end.

All of these plans for national regeneration through agriculture required assistance from big government, but none of them bear any genuine affinity to socialism. Socialists of Haggard's era aimed to abolish class divisions and private ownership of the means of production. Haggard had absolutely no sympathy for either of these goals. His objective was a system of regulated private agriculture with a mix of large and small proprietors. All proprietors must be assured of adequate supplies of labor. The fundamental motivation of his activities as an agricultural reformer was not the distress of the working class; it was the distress of the farmers. He wished to stop the rural poor from moving to the cities so that they might be available to work for honest farmers. This worry about labor supply is a constant theme of *Rural England,* Haggard's massive survey of the condition of people on the land. The attractions of higher wages and excitement in the cities were depriving farmers of the labor they needed to stay in business. Haggard stated firmly that men should not be allowed to live in rented cottages unless they gave satisfactory service as laborers for local farmers. He thought it obnoxious that farmers could not evict tenants whom they fired. He cited the example of a drunk and lazy worker who had thumbed his nose at him claiming "I don't care; I can easily get another place, and you can't turn me out of the house."[23]

Haggard was equally strong in his condemnations of wealthy financiers who mismanaged country estates which they acquired as venues for fashionable fox-hunting and partridge-shooting parties. But he proposed no draconian schemes for making them behave which are at all comparable to his strictures on farm laborers. Haggard's distaste for financiers and manufacturers arose not from any leftist sentiments, not even from a Dickensian dislike of their coarse exploitation of the workers. It arose from a backward looking tory belief in the natural superiority of the rural land-owning class. Genuine radicals and socialists could see this and marked him out as an incorrigible enemy. Haggard accepted their enmity complacently. "Their alternative," he noted, "was working for some revolution," a goal as impractical as it was undesirable.[24]

Politics in Haggard's Fiction

Once it is understood that Rider Haggard was no political maverick but a reasonably typical specimen of the Conservative "New Imperialist," a paradox arises. Nothing remotely resembling the political program of Joseph Chamberlain or Cecil Rhodes is expounded or advocated in any of his fiction. His admirers can quite plausibly argue that whatever the opinions he may have espoused as a parliamentary candidate, journalist or agricultural reformer, he did not write those opinions into his famous romances. Since his only significant impact on later generations has been achieved through those books, it follows that his other political opinions can be ignored. It is Haggard the anti-imperialist of *King Solomon's Mines* and *Allan Quatermain* that counts, not Haggard the imperialist toastmaster of the Anglo-African Writers' Club. Despite its superficial plausibility this line of argument is ultimately unsatisfying. It does not explain *why* the politics of Haggard's fiction are so different from the politics of Haggard's speeches. It glosses over the tory political statements that do appear in Haggard's less well-known realistic novels. And it does not do justice to the subtler political messages that can be detected even in the celebrated early romances. The remainder of this chapter is devoted to extracting those subtler messages.

A. Capitalism
Profit seeking characters in Haggard's fiction do not receive the glad hand of friendship which he extended to Percy Fitzpatrick and the chairman of the South African Chamber of Mines at formal banquets. The earliest novels and romances are frankly hostile to

capitalism. In *Dawn*, Haggard attributes *anti*-imperialist sentiments to businessmen. He attacks them for opposing patriotism because they deal with all national questions "as an investor deals with his funds, in order to make as much out of them as possible, not to bring real benefit to the country." *Jess* makes the same point by attributing Britain's withdrawal from the Transvaal Republic to a shopkeeper's mentality. Things would have been different if "the landed gentry and a proportion of the upper middle class" had held the reins of government. Both *King Solomon's Mines* and *Allan Quatermain* end on strongly anticapitalist notes with the rulers of Kukuanaland and Zu-Vendis pledging themselves to exclude "traders with their guns and gin," miners, "speculators, politicians and tourists." Umslopogaas regards his life as a warrior as preferable to that of financiers. "Mine is a red trade, yet it is better and more honest than some. Better is it to slay a man in fair fight than to suck out his heart's blood in buying and selling and usury after your white fashion." Haggard's other African hero, Allan Quatermain agrees. "How," he asks, "can a world be good in which Money is the moving power, and Self-interest the guiding star?"

This strident anticapitalism is modified somewhat in later works but never entirely disappears. When Haggard resuscitated Allan Quatermain in the second decade of the twentieth century, he made him a more active agent of capitalist penetration—less of a hunter and more of a trader. He never trades in gin but he does sell guns to whoever will buy them. He is on the side of big mining capital and against "illicit diamond buyers" in *Finished*. On the other hand, there are undercurrents of hostility to capital even in this later work. In *People of the Mist* an unsavory trader is given the name Rodd. The same name is given to a murderous doctor/trader in *Finished*. It calls to mind two of Cecil Rhodes' agents who were instrumental in establishing the colony of Rhodesia. One was Charles Rudd who tricked Lobengula into signing a mining concession which laid the basis for later territorial claims. The other was Dr. Leander Starr Jameson who led the abortive attack on the Transvaal in 1895. The closest Haggard ever came to creating a capitalist hero was in *Stella Fregelius*. Morris Monk makes a fortune from his invention of the aerophone, but, significantly, he is not interested in enjoying the money or in making more of it. Elsewhere, manufacturers and financiers are portrayed either as villains or maladroit parvenus.

Part of the explanation for Haggard's attitudes towards capitalism can be traced to Conservative attitudes of the 1870s which he acquired

as a young civil servant in Natal. Prime Minister Disraeli accused his
Liberal opponents of putting profit before patriotism when they attacked the wastefulness of colonies and colonial defense. Haggard accepted this analysis at face value, and wrote it into his fiction
throughout the 1880s. Later, when the "New Imperialism" had
brought about a rapprochement between high finance, Tory expansionists and ex-anti-imperialists such as Joseph Chamberlain, Haggard
softened his position.

A more fundamental source of his anticapitalism was an old-
fashioned belief in the superior moral value of landed wealth. His imagination clothed feudalism with color, humanity, and knight-
errantry. In this he resembled his youthful political hero, Disraeli.
Allan Quatermain contains the strongest statement of Haggard's
nostalgic allegiance to the feudal political and economic system.
Genuine landed aristocrats were better, "simpler," and "kinder"
than the "overbearing, purseproud" capitalists who represented the
new order. In his imaginary kingdom of Zu-Vendis he contrasted the
human face of feudalism with the cruelty of the modern English legal
system:

the law of England is much more severe upon offenses against property than
against the person, as becomes a people whose ruling passion is money. A
man may half kick his wife to death or inflict horrible sufferings upon his
children at a much cheaper rate of punishment than he can compound for
the theft of a pair of old boots. In Zu-Vendis this is not so, for there they
rightly or wrongly look upon the person as of more consequence than goods
and chattels, and not, as in England, as a sort of necessary appendage to the
latter. (153)

Haggard knew, of course, that feudalism was gone forever and that a
partnership of big government and big business was necessary for
defending the empire in the twentieth century. But that did not stop
him from indulging his romantic fantasies of ideal feudalism in his
fiction.

B. Race.

Rider Haggard's views about race as expressed in his fiction, will
not satisfy the educated sensibilities of today's world. They were,
nevertheless, far less repulsive than the opinions of most of his British
contemporaries. He did not believe that Europeans were justified in
conquering other peoples because their skins were darker or their

noses were flatter. Nor did he think that blacks were markedly inferior to whites in physique or intellect. He did, on the other hand, accept unquestioningly that whites stood higher on the ladder of civilization than blacks, that intermarriage between races was undesirable, and that where white and black lived in close association, it was natural for the light-skinned peoples to govern and be served by the dark-skinned ones.

Much of the excitement would have disappeared from his tales of African adventure if he had a postulated perfect equality between white and black. Without the assumption that the "savage" represented an earlier stage of human evolution which survived in the subconscious sections of the "civilized" white man's interior self, the essential ingredient of his psychodrama would be lacking. (It was, in fact, lacking for this very reason in the Zulu sections of the later Allan Quatermain novels.) But precisely because Haggard identified the black "savage" as a part of himself, he steered well clear of virulent racism.

The racism which does crop up in his romances is mostly a matter of color consciousness. In *She, Allan Quatermain* and *The Ghost Kings,* Haggard portrays imaginary caste-riven societies in which the darker-skinned peoples are subservient or tributary to the lighter skinned ones. He never reverses that relationship. Where heroes and heroines are black, they are usually less black than the rest of their people. Ignosi is lighter skinned than his evil rival Twala in *King Solomon's Mines.* Umbulazi is not only kinder, he is also whiter than his brother Cetshwayo in *Child of Storm.* Mameena, Nada, and Sihamba—the three outstanding female characters in Haggard's Zulu romances—are all significantly lighter and more "European" in appearance than the rest of their people. And the Zulu people are often singled out as copper colored in comparison to other black peoples. Only Umslopogaas and the dwarf Otter are portrayed as uncompromisingly black-skinned heroes.

Haggard often implies that moral superiority accompanies light colored skin. For example, "it had been a custom with Nada from childhood not to go about as do other girls, naked except for their girdles, for she would always find some rag or skin to lie upon her breast. Perhaps it was because her skin was fairer than that of other women, or perhaps because she knew that she who hides her beauty often seems the loveliest, or because there was truth in the tale of her white blood and the fashion came to her with the blood" (264—65). Men always refused to allow her to work in the field along with the rest of the women. Mameena who was similarly fair, whose hair was "curling, but not woolly," and whose "features showed no trace of the negro type," was likewise exempted from labor, as if her skin color qualified her for the cossetted existence of a middle-class English housewife.

There is a counterstrain of comment on color in Haggard's fiction which would appear on the surface to contradict these assumptions about the relationship between whiteness and morality. The deepest dyed villains in his romances are half-castes: Don José Morena in *Heart of the World* with his gang of cutthroats who are also "of mixed race and villainous appearance"; Swart Piet in *Swallow* whose face betrays "the cruelty and cunning of a black race, mingled with the mind and mastery of the white"; Hernando Pereira in *Marie* and Frank Muller in *Jess* who represent the perils of other sorts of miscegenation. All these characters are portrayed as worse than either of the races which contributed to their parentage. Why should the "whiter blood" in these characters not have the uplifting effect which it seems to have on dark heroines? The answer is that it depends on the point of view Haggard is adopting. In someone who is considered basically African, partially white ancestry and appearance are advantageous. But in someone who is considered basically white, any hint of a dark ancestry is bad.

In short, Haggard mentally arranges races on a ladder which associates light skin with superiority, but he very much prefers that these races remain "pure." Even in cases of true love, as between Foulata and Captain Good in *King Solomon's Mines* or between Allan Quatermain and Mameena in *Child of Storm*, Haggard refuses to sanction any marriage or cohabitation on the grounds that it is impossibly unacceptable to European society, and must therefore lead to the degradation of both partners. Provided that this peril is avoided, he is willing to grant every racial group its special virtues.

C. Nationality and Empire.

While Haggard never wrote tales about building or ruling the British Empire, he did write about ancient empires.

The three books he wrote about Jews under attack reveal complex, ambiguous attitudes toward nationality and empire. Haggard was barely touched by the widespread anti-Semitism of his age. Even when goaded by his friend Kipling, he refused to give credence to conspiracy theories which attributed the ills of the world to the plots of Jews and capitalists (or Jews and communists).[25] In two of his

books, *People of the Mist* and *Stella Fregelius,* rich Jews are briefly
mentioned as parvenu displacers of the old landed families, but they
are treated gently. The probable explanation for this attribute is that
Haggard believed himself to be descended from Jews as well as Danes
and shared Disraeli's fascination with the fortunes of his Jewish
ancestors since the days of Moses.

Queen Sheba's Ring (1910) describes the fall of a once powerful
kingdom of Jews in the upper Sudan. In part, it is a morality tale for
the British, warning of the fate which will overtake the nation if they
let their birthrate fall, listen to pacifist propaganda, and refuse to
draft soldiers into their armies. This lost kingdom romance is particularly interesting because Jews are cast in the unaccustomed role of
feudal agriculturalists with a marked distaste for gold and commerce.
But the most striking political message in the book is that even a
cowardly and enervated people has a right to national independence.
The would-be conquerors of the mountain kingdom are braver, wiser,
franker people, yet Haggard's adventurers throw their lot in with the
beleagured Jews.

Moon of Israel (1918) examines issues of nationalism versus empire
in a more directly imperial framework. Ana the narrator is scribe to
Seti, prince of Egypt, in the time of Moses. Majority opinion among
the rulers, priests, and people of Egypt favors both the continued
enslavement of the Jews as a labor source and the suppression of their
religion. After witnessing a particularly gross example of Egyptian
cruelty toward Jewish workers, Prince Seti undertakes to investigate
the whole Jewish question. At first he is inclined to believe that
toleration of Hebrew customs and good government could restore
amicable relations. But after experiencing the depth of the Jews'
hatred for their oppressors, he recommends that Pharaoh grant their
plea for freedom. Though Seti understands the Hebrews and marries
one of them, he does not find them lovable. They are fanatics in
religion in addition to being vengeful, devious, and avaricious.
Nevertheless he recognizes that it is too late to retain their allegiance
by toleration. Egypt must let them go.

Pearl Maiden (1903), which intertwines a love story with the events
of the final tragic Jewish uprising against Roman rule in Palestine,
describes antagonisms only a step removed from the imperial conflicts
which Haggard knew at first hand. Haggard's loyalties are divided.
He hates the avarice, self-indulgence, and tyranny of the parasitic cli-
que around the Roman emperor. At the same time, he identifies with
the honest young officer Marcus who represents the last, best remnant

of the landed gentry of the vanished Roman republic. He regrets the
self-destructive futility and fanaticism of the Jewish resisters at the
same time that he admires their valor in a just cause. Marcus
demonstrates how officers of a generous empire ought to behave
when he is sent to investigate a murder in a remote religious com-
munity. Rejecting the easy alternative of punishing everyone for one
man's crime, he makes a careful study of the people and their
customs. His report to his superiors recommends tolerance as the best
way to win the cooperation of these ignorant but essentially harmless
creatures. After negotiations have failed to mollify Jewish rebels, Marcus throws himself into battle against them with the same manly and
honorable courage. The best of Shepstone's men in South Africa
could hardly have done better.

Rider Haggard, The Novelist of Indirect Rule

The Shepstonian ideal of good imperial government was never absent from Haggard's mind when he wrote about the relations between captive nations and their conquerors. It is the conceptual link
between Haggard the "New Imperialist" of the Anglo-African
Writers' Club and Haggard the anticolonialist of *King Solomon's
Mines*. Imperial administrators of the early twentieth century called
this ideal "indirect rule."
Although the policy was initially adopted because it was cheap, it
came in the course of time to be lauded as a philosophical creed.[26] Indirect rulers believed that, within limits, the subject peoples of the
British Empire should be allowed "to develop along their own lines."
Their customs and traditions, their priests, and their rulers should be
maintained so long as they were not incompatible with the basic
moral principles of European civilization—and so long as they did not
stand in the way of Britain's basic economic and political objectives.
Theophilus Shepstone and Bishop Colenso, two of Haggard's early
exemplars, had pioneered the policy in Natal. One of Shepstone's
staff, Marshall Clarke, later applied its precepts in British Basutoland
with enough flexibility to win praise from both zealots of imperialism
and critics of empire such as the liberal economist J. A. Hobson.[27]
Haggard especially admired the capitalist magnate Sir George Goldie
who introduced something like indirect rule to the territories held by
the Royal Niger Company.[28] One of Goldie's agents, Frederick
Lugard, gave the policy its fullest, most famous expression during his
term as governor of Nigeria.

Indirect rule contains all the complexities, paradoxes, and ambiguities which characterize Haggard's writing on empire. On important occasions indirect rulers stood between non-Europeans and rapacious settlers who would have stolen their lands. In other circumstances indirect rule was used to justify the creation of labor reservoirs where outmoded agricultural methods could sustain black workers when they were not needed to work the mines, plantations, factories, or railroads of the capitalist sector of the economy. In some colonies indirect rule maintained the self-respect, language, and valued traditions of venerable kingdoms. In others it barred the rise of progressive, ambitious new groups in society while it pampered the fossilized remnants of old ruling classes.

Haggard had many reasons to like indirect rule. It was not just that it was the policy of his father figures and first tutors in government in South Africa. It was a formula which preserved the rule of "civilization" while allowing a limited arena for the intoxicating, uninhibited life of "savagery." Modern critics of colonialism are apt to remind us that in reality the "civilization" imposed by imperial government was far from disinterested benevolence, and that the lives of Africans were neither savage nor unrestrained. But that is not the way Haggard and many imperialists of his generation perceived reality. They saw an analogy between the way in which an overlay, a veneer, of civilization held uneasy sway over the wild impulses of the subconscious in European man, and the way in which the civilizing agents of Empire imposed order on barbarous peoples. Haggard was not alone in responding positively to the excitement and drama of this situation. While he cannot fairly be accused of motivating men to build empires, he may have contributed something important to the guiding ideas of men who ruled them. When Margery Perham, who was later to write the biography of the great indirect ruler Lord Lugard, set off on her first African trip in 1922, she carried just one favorite book: *King Solomon's Mines*.[29]

Indirect rule also reverberated sympathetically with Haggard's conservative politics. He believed in the superiority of the old landed aristocracy which had presided over England's gradual transition from a feudal kingdom to a constitutional monarchy. He and the indirect rulers believed that Africans should make a similarly slow transition to self-determination under the leadership of traditional chiefs. They warmed to the old elites, praising their "natural dignity" and "gentlemanly manners." They scorned the gaucheries of the up-and-coming, mission-educated Africans who strove to imitate the manners of Englishmen.

This romanticism sometimes led them to rule through corrupt, though colorful, stooges called chiefs or kings. It created enormous problems when the time came to break up Britain's African empire. But it accurately reflected the state of mind of colonial rulers who disliked parvenus at home as well as abroad and who affected to scorn the values of capitalism even as they opened the way for its expanded dominion. Haggard's novels, which discovered lost feudal kingdoms in Africa and which identified Zulu warriors with Vikings, had an immediate appeal to such people. Theophilus Shepstone was the prophet of indirect rule. Rider Haggard was its laureate.

Chapter Seven
Haggard's Legacy

Rider Haggard can no longer be dismissed as a trivial, simple-minded, or outmoded literary figure. His best work has "lived," as he predicted, not just for the devotees of light fiction but for writers of undoubted talent and power. Its importance derives from the important ideas that Haggard tackled, rather than from any innovations he made in the style or form of the novel.

The central complex of ideas which he explored arose in the wake of the Darwinian revolution. The notion that every human being possesses a dual nature had existed in Europe for centuries and had been expressed in many different forms. More recently, European intellectuals had begun to arrange the races of mankind on a vertical scale, classifying some as superior, others as inferior. Darwin's theory of evolution suggested a way of combining these two ideas. If Europeans had gradually evolved from shuffling apes to their present "superiority," then perhaps the "inferior" races of other continents represented living examples of evolutionary stages which their ancestors had passed through centuries or eons before. And if many species of animals displayed vestiges of previous evolutionary stages, then perhaps Europeans also had hidden somewhere within themselves relics of their own ancestral savage past: wild, violent elements that under certain circumstances might break loose and overwhelm the civilized elements.

Rider Haggard belonged to the first generation of Englishmen to read Darwin as adolescents uncontaminated by deep-seated prejudices. He made brilliant use of his youthful African experiences to give a literary expression to Darwinian ideas about race and evolution. In a sudden burst of creativity beginning with *King Solomon's Mines* he captured the attention of a wide audience of people who found these ideas fresh, vastly exciting, and more than a little disturbing. His significance as a figure in literary and intellectual history lies in the way he stimulated the imagination of people of his own and later generations who were gripped by the same complex of ideas. This final chapter evaluates Haggard's impact on four different groups:

social scientists; imaginative writers of his time; notable literary figures who came after him; and image makers in assorted fields of popular culture.

Late-Victorian Anthropology and Psychology

The vital link between Haggard and anthropology is Andrew Lang. Unwittingly, Haggard's own admirers have been instrumental in obscuring this link by insisting on Lang's eminence as a literary critic in order to strengthen the impact of his praise. But it was precisely because Lang was, in his own phrase, "an amateur of savages" that he was first smitten by *King Solomon's Mines*. Lang had come to anthropology through the study of classical mythology. His contribution to mythological scholarship was the suggestion that wild and apparently irrational elements in Greek myths could be explained as surviving vestiges of savage tales out of which those myths had grown. He believed that the close analysis of the myths of living savage peoples would confirm the hypothesis. This was a brilliantly simple application of Darwinian thinking to a nonbiological subject which paved the way directly for James Frazer's enormously influential application of the same approach on a grander scale in *The Golden Bough*.

These studies had led Lang to the Zulu people and their history years before he knew the name Rider Haggard. One of Bishop Colenso's clergy, Henry Callaway, had published *Nursery Tales, Traditions and Histories of the Zulus in Their Own Words* in 1868, partly with the object of demonstrating similarities between their myths and those of the European peoples. Familiar as he was with Callaway's work, Lang was thrilled to find the Zulu brought to such vivid life in *King Solomon's Mines*. And not just brought to life, but located in the same Darwinian framework that he had used in his essays on *Custom and Myth* (1884). Haggard, by equating the Zulu warriors with the Viking ancestors of Sir Henry Curtis and with the legions of the Roman Empire, was expounding in fiction the argument that Lang was pushing in his essays, that is, that living "primitive" people exemplified stages of human evolution that Europeans had passed through in previous centuries.

Because it fitted so well with popular ideas about the hierarchy of race, this idea continued to exercise a powerful influence long after professional anthropologists had abandoned the armchair evolutionary theorizing of Lang and Frazer in favor of functionalism and fieldwork among non-European cultures. Haggard's working out of the idea in his romances maintained a similarly long-standing influence because it was not viciously racist. It emphasized the kinship, albeit distant, between the African and the European rather than the gulf between them. Even anthropologists who had given up evolutionary schemes could find things to like in Haggard's work. Malinowski and the functionalist school which flourished between the world wars were often close collaborators with imperial administrators who practiced indirect rule. They could heartily agree with the sentiment expressed by Ignosi in *King Solomon's Mines* or by Sir Henry Curtis in *Allan Quatermain* that non-Europeans should as much as possible be allowed to enjoy "the comparative blessings of barbarism" free from white settlers, missionaries, and gin peddlers.

The collaboration of colonial rulers and anthropologists in touting the virtues of indirect rule is often viewed today as either cynical or naive. Terrence Ranger has called attention to the way in which administrators in Rhodesia adopted Haggard's rendition of Zulu speech and used that archaic rhetoric to perpetuate the image of Africans as primitive people, permanently confined to a a bygone era of human evolution.[1] However, not all the benefits of the policy were reserved to white men. Old African elite families gained status and sometimes wealth from their idealization by anthropologists, colonial administrators, and writers of popular literature. The Zulu royal family, among others, has escaped the proletarianization imposed on the black masses of Southern Africa by playing a role similar to that in which Rider Haggard cast it. There is even some evidence that Haggard's works have directly molded the self-image now cultivated by the scions of old African families. When Sobhuza II of Swaziland was buried in 1982, international wire services reported that his body was carried to "a hidden cave between twin peaks known as 'Sheba's Breasts.' "

Darwinian concepts of biological evolution also explain Haggard's impact on early twentieth-century psychologists, especially the founders of the psychoanalytic school. The widespread belief that vestiges of "previous stages of mental evolution" could be discerned in the psyches of modern Europeans is another example of Darwinian modes of thought applied outside the realm of biology. In his early romances Haggard gave this belief a vivid literary expression which attracted the attention of Sigmund Freud, Carl Jung, and others for reasons which are explored in chapter 3 of this book. Although Haggard eventually committed himself to reincarnation rather than evolutionary psychology as the best explanation of the "savage" elements in the human personality, those early books also attracted the attention of novelists who accepted the basic tenets of the new psychology.

Cross-Fertilization Between Haggard and Novelists of his Era

There were many different ways of dramatizing the concept of the layered personality, and Haggard was only one of a number of writers who tried their hands at it. At the same time that he was stripping away the "veneer" of civilization from white adventurers in the heart of Africa, Robert Louis Stevenson was accomplishing the same feat with drugs in *Dr. Jekyll and Mr. Hyde*. Lang perceived the similarity at once and proclaimed them brother kings of "romance." Though they never met, Haggard and Stevenson also recognized each other as pioneers carving out parallel paths in a new country.[2]

Other writers quickly followed in their footsteps. Rudyard Kipling was temperamentally and politically much closer to Haggard than Stevenson and frankly acknowledged his indebtedness. The wolf brethren of Haggard's *Nada the Lily* inspired the wolf pack of Kipling's *Jungle Book*. Kipling gave Haggard portions of the plot for the *Ghost Kings* and other romances written during the first decade of the twentieth century.[3] Morton Cohen has extensively documented their association in *Rudyard Kipling to Rider Haggard: The Record of a Friendship*.[4] That Kipling's was a much bigger talent than Haggard's goes without saying. Haggard left no equivalent to his friend's poems, songs, or portraits of low life. But on one point their interests converged—the problem of personal identity in a Darwinian universe. Kipling's occasional forays into Haggard's chosen territory took him along similar paths. The tragicomical story "The Man Who Would Be King" takes two quintessentially Kiplingesque characters through the landscape Haggard used in *Ayesha, the Return of She*. *Kim*, which was Kipling's most important exploration of the identity problem, used India as a setting, but employed Haggard's technique of immersing European characters in strange societies in order to reveal unsuspected inner characteristics. Like *King Solomon's Mines* it is a pilgrim's progress in search of identity and truth.

Another friend of Haggard's who tackled similar problems with different tools was Arthur Conan Doyle, the creator of Sherlock Holmes. Conan Doyle shared Haggard's enthusiasm for empire and the supernatural. Although Holmes operates in the dark recesses of England rather than Africa, his life is a series of quests marked by changes of identity. Drugs and disguises help him to find the truth. When Conan Doyle put Holmes aside and tried writing a novel of adventure in unknown lands, he produced books which bore the clear impress of Haggard's influence. *The Lost World,* written in 1911, resembles in many particulars *Queen Sheba's Ring* which Haggard had published the year before.

Sheba's Ring was not, as Malcolm Elwin has supposed, a reworking of *She.*[5] It was inspired by the adventures of the eccentric scholar Professor E. H. Palmer who perished in the Sinai desert while on a secret mission with Captain Gill and Lieutenant Charrington in 1882.[6] In Haggard's romance, the trio appears as Professor Ptolemy Higgs, Captain Oliver Orme, and Richard Adams. Higgs is a loud mouthed egotist who is ferocious in both academic and physical combat. Conan Doyle's *Lost World* introduces an almost identical character in the figure of the paleontologist Professor Challenger. More important than the similarity in characters, however, are the resemblances in plot and theme.

Conan Doyle sends his party of white adventurers to an unknown part of a vast continent. They have to scale steep walls and negotiate caves to enter a territory sealed off from the modern world. There they encounter primitive people with whom they identify and must share the perils of that people's perpetual struggle for life. Doyle's inspired variation on Haggard's lost kingdom romances was to make his "lost world" represent a much earlier stage in evolution and to populate it with extinct animals as well as primitive men. It opened the way for a whole subgenre of popular literature. Haggard, who was the ultimate originator of the species, later wrote his own version, *Allan and the Ice Gods* (posthumously published, 1927).

Cross-fertilization likewise occurred between Haggard and John Buchan which suggested another direction for popular literature. In the opening pages of Buchan's first successful spy thriller, *The Thirty-Nine Steps,* an innkeeper exclaims that the adventures of the fleeing hero Richard Hannay are "all pure Rider Haggard and Conan Doyle."[7] He might well have added Kipling, for Hannay, on the run from foreign agents, goes through as many changes of costume and identity as Kipling's Kim. Many other books and stories show Haggard's influence on Buchan. *Prester John,* set in South Africa, tells the story of a black rebellion led by a man supposedly descended from the Queen of Sheba whose symbol of authority is a necklace of antique diamonds. His stronghold is a vast cave in the side of an undiscovered valley surrounded by mountains. The hero is strongly tempted to give up his European identity and join the cause of this charismatic black leader. Buchan wrote many stories on the theme of Europeans who revert to pagan customs and the worship of classical gods. "The Grove of Ashtaroth," for example, follows Haggard in postulating that the Phoenician goddess Astarte was once worshipped in the depths of the African continent.[8] An Englishman who establishes a lodge there is gradually taken over by the vanished cult.

Although Haggard does not mention Buchan's stories in his memoirs or diaries (he was notoriously sensitive to suggestions of plagiarism), there is presumptive evidence that he recognized Buchan as a fellow worker in the same literary vineyard and borrowed from the younger man in his later romances. *Finished,* for example, contains not only a subplot concerning "illicit diamond buying" similar to that used by Buchan in *Prester John,* but also features a pair of degenerate villains who have built a replica of a pagan temple in the heart of the South African bush.

Influence on Later Literary Figures

Most historians of literature would be content to leave Haggard there in the general vicinity of Buchan and Conan Doyle somewhere below Kipling or Stevenson. Some of his less critical devotees wish to see him rank higher. They can and do produce evidence to support their case, most of it consisting of praise given to Haggard by later writers of undoubted quality. The praisers include D. H. Lawrence, Henry Miller, C. S. Lewis, Graham Greene, and Margaret Atwood.[9] However, if a case is to be made out for placing Haggard closer to the masters of his craft, it must be based on more than association. It is necessary to consider precisely what it is about his work that good authors have found to praise.

Without exception, they point to the same quality that impressed his contemporaries: his astonishing imagination. The characters of Ayesha and Gagool, the eerie wonders of his subterranean caverns and mountain vistas, above all the magical idea of the trek toward unsuspected marvels in the middle of nowhere—these are the things which are praised, not the skill with which Haggard translated his conceptions into words. Moreover, the twentieth-century giants all came to his books in their youth. He set their adolescent minds on fruitful lines of speculation. But he was not a model they sought to emulate in their literary maturity. Graham Greene, for example, recalls the boyish glee he felt whenever he found a novel by Rider Haggard which he had not read before. Had it not been for *King Solomon's Mines,* he speculates, "would I at nineteen have studied the appointments list of the Colonial Office?" Was it not "the incurable fascination of Gagool" that led him "to work all through 1942 in a little stuffy office in Freetown, Sierra Leone."[10]

The explanation for Haggard's popularity with serious writers is, therefore, much the same as the explanation for his popularity with ordinary lovers of "ripping yarns." He gave a unique expression to a powerful mythology which sprang up after Darwin and which still grips the imaginations of large numbers of people in all walks of life. The basic ideas that people harbor within themselves vestiges of mankind's wild primitive past, and that the discovery of those hidden facets of the personality is akin to a journey from civilized Europe into darkest Africa, can be expressed in complex "serious" literature as variously as it can in "trashy" best-sellers or movies.

One way was pointed out by Haggard's contemporary Joseph Conrad. *Heart of Darkness,* like *King Solomon's Mines,* concerns a party of adventurers on an African quest. But in contrast to Haggard's work, there is no sense of excitement or fun. The object of the quest is a person swallowed up in the unknown interior, just as it was in *King Solomon's Mines* (where Sir Henry Curtis's brother was the ostensible reason for the search). But Conrad's Kurtz has not just lost his bearings. He has lost his soul. As in *King Solomon's Mines,* the interior core of European man is equated with the African "savage." However, whereas Haggard's characters emerge shaken but refreshed from their encounter with the savage within themselves, Conrad's characters recoil with horror. Too close an approach to the heart of darkness makes then uncomfortably aware of the fragility of civilization. For all his boyish enthusiasm for Haggard, Graham Greene is more akin to Joseph Conrad in his murky stories of Africa. However, in *Journey Without Maps,* he put his finger precisely on the point which makes both Conrad and Haggard important for him, the quest for "one's place in time, based on a knowledge not only of one's present but of the past from which one has emerged."[11] Margaret Atwood, the eminent Canadian novelist, sees the same link between Haggard and Conrad: "the journey into the unknown regions of the self, the unconscious, and the confrontation with whatever dangers and splendors lurk there."[12] Haggard has a slightly different importance for writers who accepted Freudian or Jungian psychoanalytic theory as literal, rather than symbolic truth. Henry Miller's tribute to Haggard closely resembles Freud's and Jung's. He believes that Haggard really succeeded in dredging up eternal truths from within his own psyche by tapping "his unconscious with freedom and depth." Miller's own novels follow Haggard's in stressing the excitement more than the horror of the quest for the hidden essence of one's being.

It is likewise not difficult to understand why D. H. Lawrence should have remembered Haggard's work as a formative influence. Lawrence shared Haggard's disquiet at the way industrial capitalism was cutting humanity off from its roots in nature. Whatever their settings, Lawrence's novels call attention to the primitive, the dark, the Dionysiac, elemental, and energetic forces that he supposes exist within us all. Like John Buchan, he had the skill to conjure those forces out of a landscape in England, North America, or Australia and make then seem as threatening as forces emanating from ruins or jungles in Africa.

A lesser literary figure, the Jungian novelist Laurens van der Post, illustrates another way in which Haggard's influence has echoed down the corridors of twentieth-century fiction. Van der Post is a South African who knew Haggard's books as a boy and who was writing stories of Africa which reflected some of Haggard's preoccupations long before he became acquainted with the works of Jung. He was struck, during his first meetings with Jung, at the symbolic importance of Africa for the master. Jung followed Haggard in equating Africa with the primitive elements of our psyche. He was interested enough in Africa to make his own pilgrimage to the continent. He emerged, according to van der Post, with a strengthened conviction that knowing oneself thoroughly requires that the primitive within us must be acknowledged, but that one must not succumb to its attractions. "The task of modern man was not to go primitive the African way but to discover and confront and live out his own first and primitive self in a truly twentieth-century way."[13] That message, in different forms, runs through van der Post's own later books.

Rider Haggard's Influence on Twentieth-Century Image Makers of Popular Culture

Haggard lived long enough to see his influence spread far beyond the world of books. The strongly visual character of his work made it readily adaptable to motion pictures. At least eleven of his fifty-seven novels and romances have been filmed, and one of those eleven, *She,* has itself been filmed in eleven different versions. Through the motion pictures many of his brilliant inventions penetrated the consciousness of screenwriters who knew neither his name nor his books. Three distinct branches of popular culture used and reused his basic ideas: fantasy fiction, science fiction, and blood and guts adventure.

A. Fantasy

Edgar Rice Burroughs pinpointed Haggard and Kipling as the twin sources which stimulated his imagination to create Tarzan of the Jungle.[14] Sir Henry Curtis and other English aristocrats who doff their suits and dress in skins are direct forerunners of Burroughs's Lord Greystoke. The idea of a boy raised by animals comes from Kipling's *Jungle Book* which in turn was based on the wolf brethren of Haggard's *Nada.* Certain characteristics of Tarzan reflect Burroughs's peculiarly American brand of anti-intellectualism, particularly the reiterated insistence that brute force and muscle are superior to brains and education. But in the main, Burroughs's plots follow paths first opened by Haggard. One of his stories is titled "II. R. II., the Rider" and is set in a miniature kingdom. Not only does Tarzan live in Africa, but most of his adventures take the form of quests for lost tribes, lost kingdoms, lost persons, and lost treasures. The Darwinian theme of encounters with ape-men and people who stood on different rungs of the evolutionary ladder is another theme which runs through all of Burroughs's work, his Tarzan stories, his science fiction, his cavemen books, and his variations on Conan Doyle's *Lost World.* Unquestionably, Burroughs was a hack writer of extremely limited talent. However, through his enormous output of books and stories, movies, radio serials, and comic strips, he carried many of Haggard's conceptions into the mainstream of popular culture in almost every nation on earth.

Edgar Wallace performed a similar function on the other side of the Atlantic. His stories of "Sanders of the River" carry on the idealization of indirect rule in Africa which Haggard began. His story of "King Kong" fuses some of Haggard's favorite ideas—the quest into the unknown, the primitive people who worship an enormous beast (which Haggard introduced in *People of the Mist*), and the sexually motivated capture of a white woman by great apes (which Haggard used in *Allan's Wife*)—with Conan Doyle's concept of the lost world to produce a mythic rival for Mary Shelley's *Frankenstein* and Bram Stoker's *Dracula.*

Several cuts above Burroughs and Wallace as writers of fantasy
stand C. S. Lewis and J. R. Tolkien. Lewis's acknowledgment of Haggard's influence has already been noted. His use of the quest into the
unknown is the evident debt he owes. J. R. Tolkien's trilogy *The Lord
of the Rings* has been widely supposed to be rooted in his academic
knowledge of Old English, Celtic, and Nordic mythology. Robert
Giddings and Elizabeth Holland, however, in their book *The Shores
of Middle Earth*, argue that there is much evidence to indicate that
Tolkien borrowed creatively from the classics of schoolboy fiction
which he knew as a child in Edwardian England, Rider Haggard's
books among them.[15] His use of maps, the trio of adventurers, the
quest for the mines of Moria, are all reminiscent of *King Solomon's
Mines*.

B. Science Fiction

Haggard predicted in 1894 that writers of romance would eventually have to look to outer space for their settings. Africa and most of the
other continents had already been explored. "There is," he noted,
"still uncropped land in the recesses of Central Asia," but "doubtless
their harvest will soon be gathered also. Then the poor story teller,
should his imagination prove strong enough, must betake himself to
the planets."[16] He was right. Central Asia did produce one famous
imitation of *She* in James Hilton's *Lost Horizon*, but scores of Haggard's heirs are to be found chronicling adventures in interplanetary
or intergalactic space.

On first reflection it may seem strange to associate Haggard with
science fiction. His celebrated themes were vanished civilizations with
feudal social structures and little or no technology. Most people
associate science fiction with high technology and the future. Apart
from the surface glitter of rocketry and dates like 2001, however, the
new worlds of science fiction have strong affinities to the lost worlds of
Haggard's romances.

In the hands of craftsmen such as Doris Lessing or Haggard's ad-
mirer C. S. Lewis, the format can be self-consciously employed to
teach moral lessons. Once the technological problem of traversing
space is overcome, Kukuanaland, Kor, or the People of the Mist can
be as easily conjured up on Venus or Canopus as in central Africa.
Likewise, "time travel" achieves via devices such as H. G. Wells's
time machine the same sort of transformation which Haggard ac-
complished by marching a party of English gentlemen into hidden
valleys where they behave as Vikings or ancient Greeks.

Lesser science fiction writers utilize tricks and themes from Haggard's romances unself-consciously, almost automatically. They have become staples of the profession. Why should so many future worlds be organized on feudal lines? Buck Rogers no sooner steps out of his space ship on another planet than he is embroiled in the quarrels of dukes and princes. Flash Gordon is captured and led through underground caverns to meet the ravishingly lovely queen who reigns as an absolute monarch over a caste-riven society. The protagonists of Star Wars work for a "Princess" whose subjects are in rebellion against "the Empire." Much science fiction conceals nostalgia for preindustrial society between glossy covers depicting glass-domed cities on a Martian plain.

The evolutionary theme, which Haggard employed so variously in his romances, is a dominant element in twentieth-century science fiction. Edgar Rice Burroughs showed how easy it was to move the Darwinian struggle out of Africa and into space. In the same year that he dropped the infant Lord Greystoke into the jungle to be raised by apes, he teleported John Carter into the midst of warring races of Mars who carry on their struggles for survival under the watchful eyes of a corrupt priesthood of a false religion. The planet of the future turns out again and again to be a planet of the apes. Any anthology of science fiction art reveals at a glance the durability of Haggard's formula for mixing past and present in alien landscapes. Brian Aldiss's collection shows, among other things: an army of armor-clad reptilians assaulting a modern metropolis with swords and pikes; a force of giant ants issuing forth from a Grecian temple and a medieval castle; a Roman legionnaire scurrying away from exploding rockets; ape men on motorcycles among ruined megaliths; a boat load of half-naked galley slaves scaling the walls of a futuristic city; a Mayan pyramid beneath towering cliffs and a Martian sky; the "Queen of the Panther World"; a sadistic ape-king enthroned beneath soaring Gothic arches; Nordic swordsmen in Wagnerian costume at the controls of spaceships; a khaki-clad traveler on a parched desert gazing awestruck at a ruined temple; and a party of male adventurers being entertained among ionic columns, looking for all the world like Allan Quatermain, Captain Good, and Sir Henry Curtis in the land of Zu-Vendis.[17] What are all these shifts in time and changes of identity but the seeking out in future worlds of "one's place in time, based on a knowledge not only of one's present but of the past from which one has emerged"?

C. "Blood and Guts" Thriller Fiction.

A less reputable legacy derives from the violent elements in Haggard's romances. Epic descriptions of men pitted against beasts and extended accounts of savage battle earned him the sobriquet "novelist of blood." Although he greatly reduced the bloodshed in his later romances and even wrote a tract against hunting for sport (*The Mahatma and the Hare*) in 1911, his vivid images of African violence inspired a long line of imitations. Some purport to be factual accounts of Zulu life and warfare, for example, E. A. Ritter's *Shaka Zulu* and Peter Becker's *Rule of Fear*. They are, however, written without footnotes or bibliographies and emphasize the irrationality of African minds, the caprice of African rulers, and the vast loss of life in African warfare.

This image has evidently not lost its ability to titillate Western minds. It also feeds grist to the mills of reactionary propagandists in contemporary South Africa who insist that if the restraining hand of white dominance were lifted, the "tribesmen" would resume an endless round of savage warfare. The African novels of Robert Ruark and Wilbur Smith are especially potent in perpetuating that image, an image which Rider Haggard did not invent, but which he spread around the world in his tales of Allan Quatermain and Umslopogaas. Frederick Forsyth, another writer in the African blood and guts tradition, remembers Haggard as the favorite author of his childhood. Forsyth particularly recalls the violence, "the 'woodpecker,' Umslopogaas's little war axe he just pecked his enemies on the head with."[18]

Conclusion

Rider Haggard was more complex than the novels of African adventure which made him famous. His personal quest for truth and identity led through some of the most interesting new territories of European thought and action. Beginning as a Darwinian materialist in Africa on the eve of the European partition, he wound a tortuous route through colonial administration, along the fringes of literary society, downhill with the farmers of England during their worst decline in recent history, into the midst of the rogues and dreamers who rallied around Joseph Chamberlain's "New Imperialism," and out the other side into a cantankerous old age marked by dreams of reincarnation and nightmares of Bolshevik revolutions. His witness to important events and movements marks him as a character of perma-

nent interest to historians. His massive survey of the state of English
agriculture at the turn of the century will be sought out for its wealth
of empirical data long after the sociopolitical assumptions which
motivated him to make it have been dismissed as quaint evidence of
the attitudes of a dying class.

It is only his works of fiction, however, which make his living
presence felt among ordinary people at the end of the twentieth century. It is, as he anticipated, the 'romances'' penned between 1885
and 1892 which still attract a wide audience. This study has attributed
their potency to their unique metaphorical expression of late-
Victorian concepts of evolution, psychology, and anthropology whose
influence remains strongly entrenched in Western minds to the present day.

Haggard did not write the famous romances with that aim in
mind. He wrote compulsively, finding in fiction a freer outlet for the
emotional self-expression which he denied himself in every other part
of life. When he dealt with problems special to himself—the
inequities of inheritence among the landed gentry, the sufferings of
jilted young men, the search for a lost love beyond the grave—his
books were pedestrian. When he turned his imagination loose on new
ideas which disturbed other people as much as himself, he won King
Solomon's treasure.

Notes and References

Chapter One

1. Wolseley's Diary, 28 August 1875, folio WO 147/5, Public Record Office, London.
2. Lilias Rider Haggard, *The Cloak that I Left* (Ipswich, 1976), p. 24; hereafter cited as *The Cloak that I Left*.
3. Ibid.
4. H. Rider Haggard, *The Days of My Life*, 2 vols. (London, 1926) 1:1-44; hereafter cited as *Days of My Life*.
5. *Days of My Life*, 1:28-29; *The Cloak that I Left*, pp. 27-32.
6. Norman Etherington, "Why Langalibalele Ran Away," *Journal of Natal and Zulu History* 1 (1978):1-24.
7. There is no definitive biography of Shepstone. Varying judgments of the man can be found in E. Brookes and C. de B. Webb, *History of Natal* (Pietermaritzburg, 1965); J. J. Guy, *Destruction of the Zulu Kingdom* (London, 1979); and N. Etherington, *Preachers, Peasants and Politics in Southeast Africa* (London, 1978), pp. 6-23.
8. Peter Hinchliff, *John William Colenso* (London, 1964), pp. 88-89.
9. N. Etherington, "Labour Supply and the Genesis of South African Confederation in the 1870's," *Journal of African History* 20 (1979): 235-53.
10. *The Cloak that I Left*, pp. 69-75. The identity of Haggard's first sweetheart is brought to light by D. S. Higgins in his book *Rider Haggard; The Great Story Teller* (London, 1981), pp. 13-15, 33-34, 89-90.
11. Wolseley, diary, 26 May 1875, WO 147/5, Public Record Office. D. S. Higgins speculates on the slightest of evidence that Haggard had a single affair in South Africa and that his lover was a black woman: *Rider Haggard*, pp. 137-38. There would have been many opportunities for Haggard, but a genuine love affair with an African would have ruined his reputation.
12. See C. Ballard and A. Duminy, eds., *The Anglo-Zulu War; New Perspectives* (Pietermaritzburg, University of Natal Press, 1981), passim.
13. *The Cloak That I Left*, p. 90.
14. Ibid., pp. 20-21, 157-58, 279.
15. London, 1882; 3d ed. with new introduction, London, 1899.
16. Personal communication to the author from J. J. Guy.
17. *Days of My Life*, 1:211-12.
18. Haggard says six weeks in *Days of My Life*, 1:226-27, but his jotting book for 1885 notes that it was begun in January and finished 21 April 1885, folio MS 4694/2, Norfolk Record Office.
19. *Days of My Life*, 1:241.
20. Jotting Book, 1885, MS 4694/2, Norfolk Record Office.

21. Morton Cohen, *Rider Haggard, His Life and Works* (London, 1960), pp. 180-90, hereafter cited as Cohen, *Haggard*; Peter B. Ellis, *H. Rider Haggard, A Voice from the Infinite* (London, 1978), p. 119, hereafter cited as Ellis, *Haggard*.

22. Cohen, *Haggard*, p. 102; *Days of My Life*, 1:273.

23. *Days of My Life*, 1:245.

24. *Contemporary Review* (February 1887) pp. 172-80.

25. *Days of My Life*, 1:xxii.

26. *The Cloak That I Left*, p. 19.

27. H. Rider Haggard, *She and Allan* (London, 1926), p. 31.

28. Jotting Book, 1885, MS 4694/2. Norfolk Record Office.

29. *The Cloak That I Left*, pp. 72, 90, 190-91.

30. *Days of My Life*, 2:43.

31. *The Cloak That I Left*, p. 156.

32. *Days of My Life*, 2:256.

33. *The Cloak That I Left*, pp. 158, 166.

34. *Days of My Life*, 2:12, 84.

35. Ibid., 2:110-20.

36. H. Rider Haggard, *Allan Quatermain* (London, 1888), pp. 276-77.

37. P. B. Ellis, "Rider Haggard as Rural Reformer," *Country Life*, 9 December, 1976, pp. 1796-98.

38. See Haggard's preface to *Garden City and Agriculture* by Thomas Adams, (London, Garden City Press, 1905).

39. Published as *The Poor and the Land* (London, 1905).

40. Cohen, *Haggard*, pp. 191-208.

41. Jotting Book, 1895, MS 4694, Norfolk Record Office.

42. *Days of My Life*, 2:167-71. He had a fifth vision as well, in which he did not appear as a character.

43. Ibid., 2:243.

44. D.S. Higgins, ed., *The Private Diaries of Sir Henry Rider Haggard* (London, 1980), pp. 11, 21-22, 111; hereafter cited as Higgins, *Diaries*.

45. Ibid., p. 111.

46. Ibid., p. 201.

47. Ibid., pp. 163, 166, 178, 180, 189, 193-97, 201.

48. *The Cloak That I Left*, p. 253, gives a fuller extract from this entry than does *Diaries*, p. 73.

49. *The Cloak That I Left*, p. 267.

50. Higgins, *Diaries*, p. 242.

51. Ellis, *Haggard*, p. 278.

52. *The Cloak That I Left*, p. 21.

Chapter Two

1. Ruth Gordon, *Shepstone: The Role of the Family in the History of South Africa 1820—1900* (Cape Town, Balkema, 1968), pp. 88-89.

Chapter Three

1. *Days of My Life*, 1:241.
2. R. L. Stevenson, "Henry Jekyll's full statement," in *Dr. Jekyll and Mr. Hyde*, (London, Folio Society, 1948), pp. 124-27.
3. *Days of My Life*, 1:xviii.
4. See Peter Thorslev, Jr., "The Wild Man's Revenge," in *The Wild Man Within*, ed. by E. J. Dudley and E. Novak (Pittsburgh, University of Pittsburgh Press, 1972).
5. Henry Miller, *The Books in My Life* (London, P. Owens, 1952), p. 93.
6. Graham Greene, *Journey Without Maps* (Harmondsworth, Penguin, 1946), pp. 19—20.
7. Margaret Atwood, *Survival; A Thematic Guide to Canadian Literature* (Toronto, Anansi, 1972), p. 113.
8. Sigmund Freud, *The Interpretation of Dreams*, ed. James Strachey (London, Allen and Unwin, 1954), pp. 452-55. The English edition of H. Rider Haggard's novel *Heart of the World* appeared in 1896. Freud's self-analysis, mentioned in his account of the dream, began in 1897; *The Interpretation of Dreams* was finished in September 1899 (Ernest Jones, *Sigmund Freud, Life and Work* [London, Hogarth 1953], 1:293, 391).
9. The resemblance of some elements in the story to *Ruined Cities of Zululand* by H. M. Walmsley (London: Privately published, 1869) is marked. See Norman Etherington, "South African Sources of Rider Haggard's Early Romances," *Notes and Queries*, n.s. 24 (1977); 436-38.
10. H. Rider Haggard, *King Solomon's Mines* (London, 1975), p. 213.
11. From time to time, however, it has been argued that *King Solomon's Mines* is both racist and imperialist. See, for example, T. J. Couzens, "Literature and Ideology: The Patterson Embassy to Lobengula 1878 and *King Solomon's Mines*," seminar paper delivered at the Institute of Commonwealth Studies, London, 24 January 1974. In a similar vein Street, in *The Savage in Literature* (London, Routledge and K. Paul, 1975), argues that when the white party leaves, "Kukuanaland has become in spirit, if not in fact, a colony of the British Empire" (pp. 123-24). The contrary and, to me, the more convincing case is put by Alan Sandison who contends that "in this book, as in every other he wrote on Africa, he repudiates without fuss the whole arrogant notion of the white man's burden" (*The Wheel of Empire* [London, 1967], p. 31). I am in complete agreement with Sandison's reasons for denying that Haggard used the imperial situation as anything more than a striking metaphor; my views on Haggard's use of that metaphor are different.
12. This points up the distance which separates Haggard's work from much late Victorian philosophical imperialism. Materialism, the struggle for life, and the survival of the fittest are the doctrines of Haggard's villains, not his heroes.
13. Haggard, *Allan Quatermain* (London, 1888) p. 7.

14. Haggard, *She* (London, 1969), pp. 129-30.

15. C. S. Lewis, *Rehabilitations and Other Essays* (London, Oxford University Press, 1939), p. 101, thought "the shallowness and folly of the things put into the mouth of She herself and offered us for wisdom" to be the most glaring fault of the book. Lewis mistakes the function of the character. Ayesha's philosophy is meant to frighten rather than enlighten.

16. *Days of My Life*, 2:12.

17. Haggard, *Allan's Wife and Other Tales* (London, 1889), p. 150.

18. Stephen J. Gould, *Ontogeny and Phylogeny* (Cambridge, Mass., Harvard Univ. Press, 1977), pp. 115-66.

19. Haggard, *Eric Brighteyes* (London, 1893), p. 73.

20. Haggard, "About Fiction," *Contemporary Review* (February 1887), pp. 172-80.

21. *Eastern Daily Press*, 22 June 1899. Later Haggard was to call himself a "wowser", an Australian term signifying a moral puritan (*Sydney Morning Herald*, 23 April 1913). In the same speech Haggard revealed that he could see sinister tendencies in the work of others which he never discerned in his own. Speaking of romantic potboilers of his own day, he noticed that "mostly these books were written by women, and there was a large sale for them. If the ladies who turned them out quite understood what they were doing they would 'turn off the tap.' "

22. Thorslev, "The Wild Man's Revenge," especially pp. 284-85, 295-97, 302.

23. Haggard's use of Greeks in, for example, *She* and *The World's Desire*, recalls Baudet's observation that features of the eighteenth-century Indian savage were ascribed by nineteenth-century romantics to ancient Greeks. See Henri Baudet, *Paradise on Earth* (New Haven, Yale University Press, 1965), p. 50.

24. Andrew Lang, *Custom and Myth* (London, Longmans, 1884); E. D. Langstaff, *Andrew Lang* (Boston, G. K. Hall, 1978), pp. 121-36.

25. Peter Pierce has noted the importance of Haggard's aerial views in "Rider Haggard" (B.Litt. thesis, Oxford University, 1975), pp. 13-21.

26. Freud, *Complete Psychological Works* (London, Allen and Unwin, 1954) 4:122.

27. C. G. Jung, "In Memory of Sigmund Freud," in *Collected* Works of C. G. Jung (London, Routledge and K. Paul, 1966), 13:48.

28. Freud, *Interpretation of Dreams*, pp. 60, 73.

29. Jung, *Collected Works*, 13:95-96.

30. For example, "the archetype here is the participation mystique of primitive man with the soil on which he dwells, and which contains the spirits of his ancestors" (Jung, *Collected Works*, 13:82).

31. Jung, *Collected Works*, 13:87-93.

32. Jones, *Sigmund Freud*, 1:435-36.

33. A similar view is taken by Hayden White who treats the concepts of

Freud and the post-Freudians as a process of "remythification" in which the ancient fiction of the Wild Man is interiorized and once again treated as fact (*The Wild Man Within*, pp. 6-8).

34. See above, p. 1.

Chapter Four

1. Elwin, *Old Gods Falling*, pp. 256-61; *Times Literary Supplement*, 30 September 1960, p. 630; C. Hollis in *London Magazine*, n.s. 1 (1961): 87-88.

2. Cohen, *Haggard*, pp. 225-26.

3. Ellis, *Haggard*, pp. 5-6. It is also difficult "to seriously accept" that Ellis could be a competent judge.

4. Cohen, *Haggard*, 228.

5. " 'Elephant Smashing' and "Lion Shooting,' " *African Review*, 9 June 1894, p. 792.

6. At the time the book was published Haggard was accused of stealing material from W. H. Prescott's *History of the Conquest of Mexico*.

7. Higgins, *Rider Haggard*, p. 170.

8. Sol Plaatje, *Mhudi* (Lovedale, Lovedale Press, 1930). For a more general account of the period see R. Kent Rasmussen, *Migrant Kingdom* (London, R. Collings, 1978).

9. Much of Stuart's evidence is now in print as the result of the meticulous work of Colin Webb and John Wright. Successive volumes of the *Stuart Archive* are produced by the University of Natal Press.

10. Cohen, *Haggard*, 228-29. Just how far Cohen was from the truth is indicated by the Terrence Ranger's treatment of "the Rider Haggard Tradition" in "The Rural African Voice in Zimbabwe Rhodesia, Archaism and Tradition," *Social Analysis* 4 (1980): 100-15.

11. H. Rider Haggard, *Cetywayo and His White Neighbours*, 3d ed. (London, 1890), pp. 11-12; Norman Etherington, "Anglo-Zulu Relations, 1856-78," in Ballard and Duminy, *The Anglo Zulu War*, pp. 14, 32-33.

12. *A Zulu King Speaks*, ed. C. de B. Webb and J. B. Wright (Pietermaritzburg, University of Natal Press, 1977).

13. *Days of My Life*, 2:85.

Chapter Five

1. Higgins, *Rider Haggard*, pp. 99, 137, 201-2.

2. Olive Schreiner, who was infatuated with Havelock Ellis at the time Haggard made her acquaintance, did not respond to his offer of friendship.

3. Cohen, *Haggard*, p. 137; Higgins, *Rider Haggard*, pp. 40, 117, 118, 152.

4. *The Cloak I Left*, p. 17.

5. Higgins, *Rider Haggard*, pp. 63-64.

6. For an example of Haggard's antifeminist arguments, see "A Man's View of Woman," *African Review*, 22 September 1894, pp. 407-8.
7. *Days of My Life*, 1: 245-48.
8. *The Cloak That I Left*, pp. 28-29.
9. Cohen, *Haggard*, 102-14.
10. See E. J. and J. D. Krige, *Realm of the Rain Queen* (London, Oxford University Press, 1943). The foreword by Jan Smuts displays the racism associated with speculations on the alleged white ancestry of the queens. There is no other evidence to substantiate the purely European legend.
11. Above, p. 38. At the end of Goethe's *Faust*, for example, Margaret achieves apotheosis as the Eternal Feminine.
12. Above, p. 85.
13. Above, pp. 46-47.
14. Higgins, *Rider Haggard*, pp. 91-107.
15. I am indebted to the Australian psychologist Helen Winefield for first suggesting this line of speculation.
16. *Days of My Life*, 1:271-72.

Chapter Six

1. Quoted in W. L. Langer, *The Diplomacy of Imperialism* (New York, Knopf, 1951), p. 83.
2. G. N. Sanderson, "The European Partition of Africa: Coincidence or Conjuncture," *Journal of Imperial and Commonwealth History* 3 (October 1974):43.
3. Suzanne Howe, *Novels of Empire* (New York, Columbia University Press, 1949), p.20; Brian Street, *The Savage in Literature* (London, 1975), p. 14, 182-84.
4. Sandison, *The Wheel of Empire*, p. 31.
5. Ellis, *Haggard*, p. 7.
6. Cohen, *Haggard*, p. 49.
7. Higgins, *Rider Haggard* pp. 175-76.
8. *Pall Mall Gazette*, 24 April 1894, p. 8.
9. *African Review*, 21 May 1898, pp. 311-12.
10. *Standard*, 10 April and 1 May 1882.
11. *Standard*, 14 March 1883.
12. *East Suffolk Gazette*, 15 August 1899.
13. *Times*, 17 October 1899.
14. *Norfolk Chronicle and Norwich Gazette*, 4 May 1895.
15. *African Review*, 22 April 1899; *Times*, 17 October 1899.
16. *Eastern Daily Press*, 11 January, 1906; *East Anglian Daily Times*, 7 August 1906; *Spectator*, 7 October 1905.
17. Higgins, *Diaries*, pp. 218-19; above pp. 18-19.
18. R. Robinson and J. Gallagher, *Africa and the Victorians* (New York, St. Martin's, 1961), pp. 404, 460-61. See also Norman Etherington, *Theories*

of Imperialism (Totowa, New Jersey, Barnes and Noble, 1984), and B. Porter, *The Lion's Share* (London, Longmans, 1975).

19. London, 1960.

20. *Standard*, 7 November, 1905.

21. *Rural England* (London, 1902), 2: 536-39.

22. *Ibid.*, 1: 17-18, 2: 551; above p. 16.

23. *Rural England*, 1: 38-39. Haggard was aware that there was another side to the case and presented it on pages 48-49 of the same volume; but he stuck to his belief in the "tied cottage" system.

24. *Standard*, 7 November, 1905.

25. Above, p. 19.

26. For a good analysis of the problems of indirect rule, see Prosser Gifford, "Indirect Rule: Touchstone or Tombstone," in *Britain and Germany in Africa*, ed. P. Gifford and W. Lewis, (New Haven, Yale, 1967).

27. *Imperialism, A Study* (London, 1938), p. 244.

28. Higgins, *Diaries*, pp. 100-101. John Flint, *Sir George Goldie and the Making of Nigeria* (London, Oxford University Press, 1960), p. 94.

29. Obituary, *African Affairs* 81 (July 1982): 409.

Chapter Seven

1. Ranger, "The Rural African Voice," 101-113.

2. Cohen, *Haggard*, pp. 208-14.

3. *Days of My Life* 2:16-17, 208.

4. London, Hutchinson, 1965.

5. Elwin, *Old Gods Falling*, pp. 256-57.

6. See Rider Haggard, "Man Hunting in the Desert," *African Review*, 23 June, 1894, p. 842.

7. John Buchan, *The Four Adventures of Richard Hannay* (London, Hodder and Stoughton, 1933), pp. 33-34.

8. "The Grove of Ashtaroth," in *The Best Short Stories of John Buchan*, ed. D. Daniell (London, M. Joseph, 1980).

9. Cohen, *Haggard*, pp. 230-32; Ellis, *Haggard*, p. 2.

10. Introduction to *She* (London, 1957).

11. Greene, *Journey Without Maps*, (Harmondsworth, Penguin, 1946) pp. 19-20.

12. Atwood, *Survival*, p. 113.

13. Laurens van der Post, *Jung and the Story of Our Time* (New York, Pantheon, 1975), p. 51.

14. Irwin Porges, *Edgar Rice Burroughs: The Man Who Created Tarzan* (Provo, Utah, Brigham Young University Press, 1975), pp. 129-30.

15. London, 1981.

16. *African Review*, 9 June 1894, p. 762.

17. Brian Aldiss, *Science Fiction Art* (London, New English Library, 1975), pp. 14, 15, 20, 30, 35, 54-57, 59, 79, 93, 98.

18. *Sunday Times*, 22 August 1982.

Selected Bibliography

J. E. Scott's *Bibliography of the Works of Sir Henry Rider Haggard 1856-1925* (Bishops' Stortford, England: Elkin Mathews Ltd., 1947) is still the starting point for students and scholars. It should be used in conjuction with the good bibliographies in the books by Ellis and Higgins listed below under Secondary Sources.

PRIMARY SOURCES
There is no standard edition of Haggard's works. In this list the original edition is given except when a more accessible edition has been used in the preparation of this book. In the latter cases the date of first publication is indicated in parentheses.

1. Fiction

Allan and the Ice-Gods. London: Hutchinson, 1927.
Allan Quatermain. London: Longmans, Green, 1888 (1887).
Allan's Wife. London: Spencer Blackett, 1889
The Ancient Allan. London: Cassell, 1929 (1920).
Ayesha. London: Ward Lock, 1905.
Beatrice. London: Longmans, Green, 1890.
Belshazzar. London: Stanley Paul, 1930.
Benita. London: Cassell, 1906.
Black Heart and White Heart and Other Stories. London: Longmans, Green, 1900.
The Brethren. London: Cassell, 1904.
Child of Storm. London: Cassell, 1913.
Cleopatra. London: Longmans, Green, 1889.
Colonel Quaritch VC. London: Longmans, Green, 1889 (1888).
Dawn. London: Longmans, Green, 1896 (1884).
Eric Brighteyes. London: Longmans, Green, 1891.
Fair Margaret. London: Hutchinson, 1907.
Finished. London: Ward Lock, 1917.
The Ghost Kings. London: Cassell, 1926 (1908).
Heart of the World. London: Macdonald, 1954 (1896).
Heu-Heu. London: Hutchinson, 1924.
The Holy Flower. London: Ward Lock, 1915.
The Ivory Child. London: Cassell, 1916.
Jess. London: Smith, Elder, 1887.
Joan Haste. London: Longmans, Green, 1895.
King Solomon's Mines. London: J. M. Dent, 1975 (1885).
The Lady of Blossholme. London: Hodder & Stoughton, 1909.

Love Eternal. London: Cassell, 1918.
Lysbeth. London: Longmans, Green, 1901.
The Mahatma and the Hare. London: Longmans, Green, 1911.
Maiwa's Revenge. London: Longmans, Green, 1888.
Marie. London: Cassell, 1912.
Mary of Marion Isle. London: Hutchinson, 1929.
Mr. Meeson's Will. London: Spencer Blackett, 1888.
Montezuma's Daughter. London: Longmans, Green, 1893.
Moon of Israel. London: John Murray, 1918.
Morning Star. London: Cassell, 1910.
Nada the Lily. London: Macdonald, 1949 (1892).
Pearl-Maiden London: Longmans, Green, 1903.
The People of the Mist. London: Longmans, Green, 1919 (1894).
Queen of the Dawn. London: Hutchinson, 1925.
Queen Sheba's Ring. London: Macdonald, 1953 (1910).
Red Eve. London: Hodder & Stoughton, 1911.
She. London: Macdonald, 1969, (1887).
She and Allan. London: Hutchinson, 1926 (1921).
Smith and the Pharaohs. Bristol: J. W. Arrowsmith, 1920
Stella Fregelius. London: Longmans, Green, 1904.
Swallow. London: Longmans, Green, 1899.
A Tale of Three Lions. London: John W. Lovell, New York, 1887.
The Treasure of the Lake. London: Hutchinson, 1926.
The Virgin of the Sun. London: Cassell, 1922.
The Wanderer's Necklace. London: Cassell, 1914.
The Way of the Spirit. London: Hutchinson, 1906.
When the World Shook. London: Cassell, 1919.
Wisdom's Daughter. London: Hutchinson, 1923.
The Witch's Head. London: Maxwell, n. d. (1884).
The Wizard. London: J.W. Arrowsmith, 1896.
The World's Desire. London: Longman's Green, 1890.
The Yellow God. London: Cassell, 1909.

2. Non-Fiction
Cetywayo and His White Neighbours. London: Trubner, 1882
    (edition with new material printed in 1888).
The Days of My Life. London: Longmans, Green, 1926.
Dominions Royal Commission, 24 vols, HMSO, 1912 to 1917.
A Farmer's Year, Being His Commonplace Book for 1898. London:
    Longmans, Green, 1899.
My Fellow Labourer and The Wreck of the Copeland. New York:
    George Munro, 1888.
A Gardener's Year. London: Longmans, Green, 1905.
The Poor and the Land. London: Longmans, Green, 1905.

Regeneration: Being an account of the Social Work of the Salvation Army in Great Britain. London: Longmans, Green, 1910.
Report on the Salvation Army Colonies (Royal Commission), HMSO, June 1905.
Royal Commission on Coast Erosion, 3 vols, HMSO, 1907, 1909 and 1911.
Rural Denmark. London: Longmans, Green, 1911.
Rural England. London: Longmans, Green, 1902.
A Winter Pilgrimage. London: Longmans, Green, 1901.

SECONDARY SOURCES

Selected
Cohen Morton. *Rider Haggard, Life and Works*. London: Hutchinson, 1960. This was the first biographical study by an academic critic. It exaggerated Haggard's failings as a literary stylist and did not explore the deeper meanings of his fiction. Nevertheless, it is worth reading because of the extensive research Cohen conducted among reviewers of Haggard's work.
Cohen, Morton. *Rudyard Kipling to Rider Haggard*. London: Hutchinson, 1965. This annotated collection of correspondence documents the close relationship between the two men in literature and politics.
Ellis, Peter B. *Rider Haggard, A Voice from the Infinite*. London: Routledge and Kegan Paul, 1978. This is not a scholarly work and should be used with caution. Its bibliographies are useful.
Elwin, Malcolm. *Old Gods Falling*, London: Hutchinson, 1939. This is a typical example of the drubbing Haggard received from most critics in the inter-war years.
Etherington, Norman. "South Africa Origins of Rider Haggard's Early African Romances," *Notes and Queries*, n.s. 24 (October 1977): 436-38. This provides information on the historical background to some of Haggard's tales.
Greene, Graham. *The Lost Childhood and Other Essays*. A landmark in the revival of Haggard's reputation. London: Eyre & Spottiswooode, 1954.
Haggard, Lilias Rider. *The Cloak That I Left*. London: Hodder & Stoughton, 1951. This book includes some but not nearly all of the undocumented family legends about Haggard and his kin.
Higgins, D.S., *Rider Haggard, The Great Storyteller*. London: Cassells, 1981. This work is short on literary analysis but contains a good deal of previously unpublished information on Haggard's life.

Higgins, D.S. ed. *The Private Diaries of Rider Haggard.* London, Cassells, 1980. Unfortunately, this truncated edition of some of Haggard's voluminous diaries (begun in 1914) is of limited value because the editor does not indicate where words and entries have been omitted.

Ranger, Terrence. "The Rural African Voice in Zimbabwe Rhodesia: Archaism and Tradition," *Social Analysis* 4 (September, 1980): 100-15. Ranger, one of the most distinguished of modern African historians shows how Haggard's rendition of Zulu speech patterns was adopted by British colonial administrators.

Sandison, Alan. *The Wheel of Empire.* London: Macmillan, 1967. Sandison's chapter on Haggard is serious, subtle and should be read by every student of his novels.

Index